Keep the Flame
Burning
in your
MINISTRY

IVAN L. WILLIAMS, SR.

Keep the Flame
Burning
in your
MINISTRY

Addressing passion, burnout, and renewal in pastoral ministry

Brighter Hope
MINISTRIES

"Fostering hope and a future for today's generation"

Keep the Flame Burning In Your Ministry:
Addressing passion, burnout, and renewal in pastoral ministry.

For informational, educational, ministry, or promotional sales use please write or visit us online. Brighter Hope Ministries, P. O. Box 293043 Sacramento, California 95829-3043. www.brighterhope.org

FIRST EDITION 2004

Williams, Sr., Ivan L., 1963-
    Keep the flame burning in your ministry: Addressing passion, burnout, and renewal in pastoral ministry / Ivan L. Williams, Sr.
    ISBN 0-9752913-3-5

Edited by A. Jeanice Warden
Cover design by Davis Designs & D. T. Graphics and Design
Book design & typesetting by D. T. Graphics and Design

1 2 3 4 5 6 7 8 9 10 00

"This book is both eye opening and life changing for the minister. In an age when many are suffering from fruitless ministry and emptiness on the inside, Dr. Williams gives voice to the cry of the pastor's heart. It describes a state that several are in and are not yet aware and also a state that many are headed towards if left to their own devices. Dr. Williams speaks to the facets of ministry that are unique to Seventh-day Adventist ministers. He addresses this problem of burnout but also shares pertinent prevention measures and practical prescriptions for renewal. This book is a must-have for ministry."

Andrea Trusty King, M.Div.
Associate Pastor, Thirty-first Street SDA Church
Vice President, Brighter Hope Ministries, San Diego, CA

"Williams has written a book that every pastor, church administrator, and seminary professor should read, digest, and grow from. Far from merely presenting another work describing the relevance and prevalence of pastoral burnout, he goes deep to the root of the issues that cause burnout and then seeks to encourage his readers to a more biblically balanced lifestyle as a way of prevention and renewal. I found his book to be disturbingly accurate and liberating as I was forced to relive those days as a young pastor when I felt that I might have been on the verge of burnout. An excellent resource!"

E. Dean Peeler, D.Min.
Pastor, Dupont Park SDA Church, Washington, D.C.

"In a time when pastors and their families are flaming out at a record pace, Ivan L. Williams' treatment of the oft-neglected issues contributing to pastoral burnout, and the suggested processes to revitalize passion for ministry is immensely practical and Biblically-based. What a grand investment of time for those of us thirsty to rekindle passion and joy in ministry!"

Cleveland Hobdy, III, Ph.D.c.
Pastor, Love of Life Fellowship, Federal Way, WA

7

"Fostering hope and a future for today's generation"

P.O. Box 293043
Sacramento, CA 95829-3043
Visit us online at:
www.brighterhope.org

DEDICATION

To Kathleen, Imani, and Ivan, II

**God's will and purpose is so dear and clear,
because of you!**

CONTENTS

CONTENTS

ACKNOWLEDGEMENTS

It is impossible to state how incredibly significant the gems of mentorship, training, and fellowship with other pastors has meant to me over my 18 years in pastoral ministry. Simply put, my journey has been greatly enhanced by pastors and church members who cared enough to disclose and share their own successes and failures to me early in my pastoral ministry.

The completion of this book would not have been possible without the Holy Spirit's impressive unction. I praise Jesus for being my Saviour and for being the Greatest Example and Witness of balance in ministry (Luke 2:52). I also praise God for the incredible support and patience of my beautiful wife Kathleen, my daughter Imani, and my son Ivan, II. I thank the Lord for the continued inspiration of my parents, Julian and Wilhelmena Williams, for my brother, Shawn and his belief and support in me, for the encouragement of my father and mother-in-law, Robert and Yvonne Scott, and for the rest of my family who have stood in the gap through prayer.

I would also like to acknowledge the following people and organizations for their friendship, encouragement, training, support, and visionary stimulation. Dr. Eric Moore, Hallerin Hill, Joe Holder, Pastor Melvin Preston, Geneviene Beenen, Pastor Anthony Paschal, Dr. Ernie

Furness, Drs. Leslie and Prudence Pollard, Leola Wade, Geraldine Maddox, Pastor Stephen Henderson, Pastor Richard Long, Sr., Dr. Nosakhere Thomas, Wyatt Phillips, Pastor Gregory Johnson, Dr. Roland Hill, Dr. James Kyle, Pastor David Richardson, Jr., Pastor Calvin Watkins, Dr. Barry Black, Pastor James Robins, Dr. Delbert Baker, Pastor Calvin Robinson, Sr., Pastor Ronald Pollard, Pastor and Mrs. Lawrence Witherspoon, Mark Washington, William Brown, Doris Gully, San Diego Maranatha Seventh-day Adventist Church Family, Sacramento Capitol City SDA Church Family, and Pine Springs Ranch. Finally, this book would not be complete if it were not for A. Jeanice Warden, my editor, and Beverly McGhee, the typesetter and graphic designer. I am forever indebted to you both; a thank you is not enough.

INTRODUCTION

THE FUEL
Pastoral Passion

"There is no passion like that of a functionary for his function."

— Georges Clemenceau —

Moses saw that though the bush was on fire it did not burn up. So Moses thought, "I will go over and see this strange sight — why the bush does not burn up." When the LORD saw that he had gone over to look, God called to him from within the bush, "Moses! Moses!" And Moses said, "Here I am." "Do not come any closer," God said. "Take off your sandals, for the place where you are standing is holy ground."

Exodus 3:2b-5

THE FUEL
Pastoral Passion

…His word is in my heart like a fire,
a fire shut up in my bones.
I am weary of holding it in; indeed, I cannot.

Jeremiah 20:9

This book is about vibrant staying power in pastoral ministry. I wrote it to encourage pastors to live a balanced life, free from burnout, and to live increasingly with a passionate yearning for God and His people. Since pastors do burnout, this book will also render a process for renewal. Pastors minister often in these contemporary times submerged beneath the pendulum effect of legitimate crises—to repetitive pettiness—to the awesome highs that accompany positive life changing spiritual intervention. Therefore, through the ministerial journey, pastors soon find out that the feeling of personal fulfillment, immediate satisfaction, or the sense of accomplishment is not always the end. However, it has been my experience that personal fulfillment is yielded while remaining faithful in the midst of the demands, expectations, and stresses of ministry.

Pacing one's self, balancing a personal life, and finding the appropriate priority of vocation are daily concerns in the sojourn of pastors. Imbalance among these priorities often results in frustration, discouragement, and even burnout. Although maintaining passion, preventing burnout, and discussing methods of renewal among pastors is real in most denominations, this book will view these issues through the scope of Seventh-day Adventist pastoral ministry. It addresses the need for a greater passion among pastors, the potential causes of burnout in pastoral ministry, as faced in the Seventh-day Adventist Church, and discusses methods of burnout prevention and ways Adventist pastors can renew themselves.

Pastoral passion wanes when the melodious chords of heaven's musical mandate are drowned out by the beat of today's pace. Pastors and congregations are significantly time-starved, and its effect causes significant sorting, sifting, and a re-evaluating of priorities. In the midst of this fast paced society, even the makers of Tylenol pain relievers are targeting busy people who have no time to get sick, and they promise the pain to be relieved in just minutes. According to Jonathan D. Salant of the *Associated Press*, motorists in cities across America spend well over an average of 36 hours a year just sitting in motor vehicle traffic. This does not even include commuting time. Couple this with a suffocating personal schedule and add to it unrealistic expectations and demands; it is easy to develop an overwhelming sense of having to always try and catch up. Pastors lose passion when the busyness of ministry drowns out the purpose and meaning for which they serve.

My first pastoral assignment was in Charlotte, North Carolina in 1985. Looking back, school could not prepare me at 21 years of age for the reality of front line everyday pastoral

> *Pastors lose passion when the busyness of ministry drowns out the purpose and meaning for which they serve.*

ministry. I have learned that only the doing of ministry, or standing in the gap between God and His people, can truly give a real sense of understanding, meaning, and purpose in response to God's calling in my life. Changing the world all by myself was my motto, and I would dare say probably is the motto, dream, and goal of every theological student coming out of educational training. I will never forget the first full day of ministry that required my complete attention in time, prayer, and effort. I conducted a funeral in the morning and presided over a wedding ceremony in the afternoon. It gave me a great sense of ministry and definitely reminded me of my absolute inability to minister without total dependence upon my Saviour. My eyes were opened on that day. Robert H. Ramey, Jr. in his book Thriving in Ministry, describes in a clearer sense what my eyes being opened on that day really meant and means for others today. He shares a sermon from a former student that preached about what he did not share with her regarding ministry while in the seminary. The sermon is entitled, "Dear Bob:"

> *"You forgot to tell me that ministry means spending hours in the emergency room with a virtual stranger, passing cast padding to an orthopedist I've never met, and trying to be an advocate for somebody who needs one desperately.*
>
> *You forgot to tell me that ministry means I'm supposed to know what to do when I get six or eight phone calls from people in varying degrees of hysteria, all of whom want me to fix the fact that people are doing things which can best be described as lewd and lascivious on the church property in broad daylight.*
>
> *You forgot to tell me that there aren't enough boxes on the calendar for all the things that need to get done.*
>
> *You forgot to tell me that there would be days when I would strongly suspect that I'm the only one around here who knows how to put a new roll of toilet paper in the bathroom.*

You forgot to tell me that sometimes people wouldn't say what they really mean, and you forgot to tell me how I'm supposed to know when that's happening.

You forgot to tell me that I can't do it all myself, that I can't make all of the people happy all of the time, and that people can't always do the things they say they will.

And while we're at it, Bob, you forgot to tell me how to say No!" [1]

Is it the all consuming and at times overwhelming job of pastoral ministry that blows the pilot light of passion out? As a pastor, does your passion for God and His people dwindle away at times? Can pastors remain or even grow more passionate about the Lord and their calling? Has the flame burning at the bush of your heart grown dim? The Bible is true! We should not boast about tomorrow, because we do not know what the day will bring *Proverbs 27:1*. But thanks be to God who we know holds tomorrow.

Moses exemplifies for us what it means to have a pastoral heart filled with passion for his God and his people.

I have not really defined pastoral passion yet, but if I were to describe it, Moses would be a great example. Moses exemplifies for us what it means to have a pastoral heart filled with passion for his God and his people. Let's go to holy ground and meet Moses at the place where he met the God of Abraham, Isaac, and Jacob. The Bible says:

> *Now Moses was tending the flock of Jethro his father-in-law, the priest of Midian, and he led the flock to the far side of the desert and came to Horeb, the mountain of God. There the angel of the Lord appeared to him in flames of fire from within a bush. Moses saw that though the bush was on fire it did not burn up. So Moses thought, "I will go over and see this strange sight – why the bush does not burn up." When the Lord saw that he had gone over to look, God called to him from within the bush, "Moses! Moses!" And Moses said, "Here I am." "Do not come any closer," God said. "Take off your sandals, for the place where you are standing is holy ground." Exodus 3:1-5*

Moses' encounter with the Lord bears witness to all that serve in ministry. The impetus to follow God's leading and the heart of passion to go forward in service is solely ignited by the initiating contact of the Divine. God's Word in my mouth, God's call on my life, and God's unction to go where He leads is the only sure source of passionate staying power in pastoral ministry. Serving for anything else or for any other reason will not sustain you. Disappointment, despair, and discouragement will only be the result. Think about it! God made contact with Moses. God chose Moses. God initiated contact with Moses to solicit his faithful service for the deliverance of the chosen people of Israel. The passionate flame of ministry is only as great as the continual encounter at the bush with God. God is the source of the continual flame burning in my heart. When disconnected from the source of the fire, the flame grows dim. The longer the pastor stays away from the holy ground the more disillusioned the journey.

> *"The divine command given to Moses found him self-distrustful, slow of speech, and timid. He was overwhelmed with a sense of his incapacity to be a mouthpiece for God to Israel. But having once accepted the work, he entered upon it with his whole heart, putting all his trust in the Lord. The greatness of his mission called into exercise the best powers of his mind. God blessed his ready obedience, and he became eloquent, hopeful, self-possessed, and well fitted for the greatest work ever*

given to man. This is an example of what God does to strengthen the character of those who trust Him fully and give themselves unreservedly to His commands.

A man will gain power and efficiency as he accepts the responsibilities that God places upon him, and with his whole soul seeks to qualify himself to bear them aright. However humble his position or limited his ability, that man will attain true greatness who, trusting to divine strength, seeks to perform his work with fidelity. Had Moses relied upon his own strength and wisdom, and eagerly accepted the great charge, he would have evinced his entire unfitness for such a work. The fact that a man feels his weakness is at least some evidence that he realizes the magnitude of the work appointed him, and that he will make God his counselor and his strength."[2]

In *Numbers 14:1-10,* Moses exemplifies for every pastor the great witness of passion so strong for the Lord to do what is right in the midst of opposition from public opinion and pressure. Later on in chapter fourteen of Numbers Moses pleads with the Lord as a type of intercessor for Israel. Not only did the Lord desire to disinherit His chosen people and build another great nation, but He also desired to destroy Israel. Moses asked the Lord to pardon their iniquity stemming from unbelief, and God pardoned Israel according to the word of His faithful servant (pastor) Moses. Seeking the presence of God has given me an express sense of clarity about His will and purpose for my life. His will is best and His purpose is always sure. To whom God calls, He equips and enables. Since God initiates the call to pastors, He places His Word in their mouths, *Jeremiah 1:9*, He also equips them with gifts *1 Corinthians 12*, and promises to finish what He starts in them, *Philippians 1:6*. Keeping the flame burning in pastoral ministry is maintained through the faithful trust connection and total dependence on the Lord. Therefore, pastoral passion is defined as the intense driving desire to live out and practice God's expressed will and purpose in your life.

> *Pastoral passion is defined as the intense driving desire to live out and practice God's expressed will and purpose in your life.*

The heart of the Spirit-filled pastor is one that cares for the flock (congregation) through sacrificial guidance and faithful service. Only a continual yearning and striving for spiritual depth, meaning, and purpose can fan the singed embers of pastoral ministry into passionate flames once again. Like Moses, we must desire to seek holy ground and be attracted to God's awesome presence. It is only in His presence that we receive direction, instruction, and fresh springs of living water to continue on the desert journey in ministry.

One cannot truly discover real meaning and purpose or even answer the question why we do, what we do in ministry unless we maintain a depth in our spiritual life through prayer and the study of God's Word. A daily walk with Jesus Christ fuels all relevant life changing preaching, the casting of spiritual vision, courageous administrative leadership, and compassionate service.

As a pastor I am sure you would agree wholeheartedly with our Lord, that the harvest is great but the laborers are few. Ironically, while writing this book, someone is in need of prayer, counseling, a sermon of hope, relationship counseling, help settling a conflict, anointing, healing, visitation, salvation, shall I continue? The harvest is great, but just to know the Lord of the harvest, makes the labor worth it all. Flaming out does not have to be an option. The pace in ministry may wear you thin, but fresh sparks from heaven are available to the pastor who desires a steady flourishing source of passionate zeal that stands against the extinguishers of your visionary flame. Maybe you can say along with me, that after years of pastoral ministry you still love taking off your shoes at the burning bush in the presence of the Holy One.

The examination of the potential causes of burnout in Seventh-day Adventist pastoral ministry may be first related to the pastors inappropriate response to the great gospel commission. Adventist pastors' sense of personal or general church mission may be inappropriate or unrealistic. Second, burnout among Adventist pastors is related to their inability to find a balance in relationship to conference, congregation, community, and home life. Inevitably, this will cause personal dilemmas that may be internal and/or external. Third, burnout among Adventist pastors is related to their ability or inability to handle relational conflict.

Understanding potential causes of burnout, and recognizing its signs and symptoms are essential to its prevention, and equally essential in the restoration of pastors who have become its victims. Therefore, to prevent burnout, the Adventist pastor must be made aware of the potential causes of burnout. For those pastors who have suffered burnout they must understand the healing aspects for renewal, restoration, and revival.

In this book, Chapter one clearly defines burnout and renewal as it relates to pastoral ministry. It gives Biblical examples and describes burnout symptoms.

Chapter two provides possible causes of burnout in the

pastoral ministry of the Seventh-day Adventist Church and describes the plight of pastors as it relates to the demands of their jobs. This chapter also emphasizes balance in the journey of ministry through the pastors' professional and personal lives.

Chapter three describes and defines what it means to be a Seventh-day Adventist pastor by looking at the Bible and the Adventist history of the pastorate. This chapter also speaks to the issue of being hired or called. And closes by addressing and defining an Adventist term called "finishing the work."

Finally, Chapter four emphasizes the resources that are available to Adventist pastors in particular, (but available to all) to be used as a prescription for burnout prevention. This chapter also gives a strategy of renewal for the pastors who have experienced burnout, and yet desire to thrive once again in ministry. It is my prayer that as you read this book, you will be encouraged to maintain a passionate zeal in your pastoral ministry, be made aware of the signs and symptoms of burnout, and to be given practical steps for prevention and spiritual principles for renewal.

CHAPTER

FLAMING OUT
Addressing Pastoral Burnout

"Be patient with everyone,
but above all with thyself."

— Francis De Sales —

"Receive him therefore in the Lord with all gladness, and hold such men in esteem; because for the work of Christ he came close to death, not regarding his life, to supply what was lacking in your service toward me."

Philippians 2:29, 30 NKJV

FLAMING OUT
Addressing Pastoral Burnout

The righteous will flourish like a palm tree,
they will grow like a cedar of Lebanon;
planted in the house of the LORD,
they will flourish in the courts of our God.
They will still bear fruit in old age,
they will stay fresh and green…

Psalms 92:12-14

Burnout is not a term or phenomenon that is new to contemporary times, but it is a recurring issue in the work of the ministry, and therefore needs to be addressed. What causes burnout? What about the work of pastoral ministry causes ministers to burn out? What spiritual solutions or practical steps, if any can be taken to prevent burnout? Is there any hope of renewal for the pastor experiencing burnout? Can passion and zeal for ministry be rekindled? Do not be discouraged if you do not have the answers on your own, but continue to read on and you will find the answers.

In <u>Webster's New Ninth Collegiate Dictionary</u> burnout is defined as "exhaustion of physical or emotional strength."[1] Ralph Douglas Haynes in his thesis entitled "An Outline of Clergy Depression with Suggested Procedures and Strategies for Healing," reflects on three illustrations of the use of the word burnout by referring to the devastation of a fire. These three illustrations are exemplified as: a burned building gutted by a devastating fire; a circuit breaker overloaded and blown, no longer able to carry currents; and lastly, a forest devastated by fire, unable to restore itself.

Reflecting on an empty building gutted by a devastating fire, Haynes observes that burnout is like an empty shell with nothing left but walls. In comparison, the burned out individual feels empty, having all internal resources burned away with nothing left to offer in ministry but external manifestations. This is the act of simply going through the motions, without emotion or passion for the work of the ministry. He suggests that this may be the result of emptiness.[2] By nature, the job of pastors requires that they give of their time; it is a helping profession. In order to continue giving and helping, pastors must be recharged and renewed personally. This can be done through participation in non-work related activities, vacations, physical exercise, relaxation, and through the spiritual rekindling of their own personal walk with God. I have found that interpersonal reflection and

> *Admittedly, without addressing the internal person, the pastor simply will function externally; practicing a ministry that is hollow and empty.*

self-disclosure to trusted colleagues has greatly helped me along my pastoral journey. Admittedly, without addressing the internal person, the pastor simply will function externally; practicing a ministry that is hollow and empty.

Haynes also compares burnout to destructively high temperatures that have caused electrical circuits to overload and blow, causing all circuit breakers to melt the electrical wires, and making them incapable of carrying any currents. Here the person who experiences burnout is left helpless to continue functioning in a normal manner. The circuits are gone, and they can no longer expend the energy necessary for the task, but they continue on. Haynes suggests, that by the person pressing on, he/she may be in a state of helplessness.[3] Many Adventist pastors find themselves trapped in this vicious cycle of continuing on in ministry with nothing more to give. They really wish that they could leave pastoral ministry, but because of educational training, years in service, and the fear of financial loss they remain in ministry. They have no creative ideas to give, no visions for direction to render, and no desire to emphasize mission. They continue on because it is all that they know, and it is all that they have been trained to do. Many remain in ministry years after the passion has dissipated, simply because of their fear of not being able go find other employment and of being perceived as a failure. Others remain in pastoral ministry because they personally believe that to leave is to forsake their calling by God.

Lastly, Haynes sees burnout as relating to a forest fire so intense that it destroys everything, including the life giving humus, leaving the forest without the capacity to restore itself. Haynes equates this with a sense of hopelessness within the pastor.[4] Some pastors leave ministry never to return. Some even become so disillusioned that they leave the church of their denomination. Intense ministry for the Adventist pastor must be followed up with intense debriefing and deliberate efforts of seeking help. It is very important that pastors get help along their pastoral journey and long before this stage in their work.

> *Burnout is therefore defined as a multi-faceted experiential feeling of exhaustion. It is felt physically, mentally, emotionally, and spiritually.*

Burnout is therefore defined as a multi-faceted experiential feeling of exhaustion. It is felt physically, mentally, emotionally, and spiritually. It drives the pastor to care for nothing and even robs the desire to be cared for. It causes feelings of negativity and feelings of numbness, and may lead to depression.[5] Burnout as described in these patterns of experiences and characteristics involves the body, mind, and spirit,[6] which equals the total person. Because burnout is real in pastoral ministry, so is the renewal and recovery from it. Renewal from pastoral burnout is essential to the hope and assurance of those called to ministry in times of ever-increasing demands.

BURNOUT SYMPTOMS

Understanding pastoral burnout and its symptoms is crucial in its recognition. Otherwise, as Harold Scott says, "pastors who are experiencing a degree of burnout may actually encounter the term and related discussion, but make no connection to their own personal situation."[7]

Gary Collins, a professor of pastoral counseling and psychology at Trinity Evangelical Divinity School, expressed this importance by stating, "burnout is a common–though often unrecognized–condition of Christian people–helpers."[8] Recognition is important because if burnout remains unrecognized, it will continue to damage and destroy the vision, vitality, and zeal of the pastor. In 1982 John A. Sanford wrote that burnout had become enough of a problem that it attracted the attention of professionals like behavioral scientists, who identified certain typical symptoms of the condition of burnout as "difficulty in sleeping; somatic complaints such as weight loss, lack of interest in food, headaches and gastro-intestinal disturbances; a chronic tiredness of the sort that is not repaired by sleep or ordinary rest and only temporarily alleviated by vacations; low-grade, persistent depression; and a nagging boredom."[9]

I agree with William H. Willimon's perspective on workers in the church that appear to be burned out. He does not necessarily see church workers burned out from overwork, as much as from their being overburdened with the trivial and the unimportant.[10] He also suggests that burnout comes when our commitment dissipates and the smallest tasks like visiting prospective church members, attending board meetings, and filling out evangelism reports become drudgery.[11] For Willimon, in the world of work, burnout occurs when energy is expended without fuel being added. In his opinion, "The fuel that supplies the energy to minister as clergy or lay ministers is a conviction that what we do has meaning. Energy to stay committed arises out of meaningful attachments. When we no longer find meaning in what we do, even the smallest action drains us. Burnout is the result of a lack of meaning."[12]

Burnout is the result of a lack of meaning.

Brooks Faulkner, describing burnout in pastors professional lives states,

At its very worst, burnout occurs when there is really nothing that the person cares about. He goes to his work without any symptoms of optimism. Negative feelings consume the thought processes. He feels depressed. He doesn't really want to be around the people he works with, but the strange part of it is he doesn't want to be away from people all that much either. Nothing satisfies his wants and needs. He feels torn apart. He begins to treat people in a dehumanizing way. They are simply a necessary part of getting through the day. Compassion is difficult if not impossible.

He feels put down by others. He feels put upon by persons who seek favors or who want something from him. He begins to feel so used that he suspects others only do him favors for what they can get out of him at a later time.[13]

This description is an excellent example of the condition called burnout, because it gives us a much better understanding of how far this problem can go in the life of a pastor. The potential of burnout must be faced and addressed in the everyday life of the Adventist church pastor. Therefore, it is necessary for pastors to implement measures of prevention and communicate openly to their congregations about delegating in ministry. This will help to bring awareness to this issue.

G. Lloyd Rediger suggests that burnout is a "version of the depressive syndrome, but it is unusual enough to require specialized attention and treatment."[14] Some signs of burnout include increased irritability or becoming easily annoyed and distracted, losing enthusiasm for ministry tasks, and complaining about not being appreciated. Other signs include sporadic efforts such as the increase of days filled with highs and lows. For example, going all out on one task and failing to complete the next task without reason. Another advanced sign of burnout is hostility and cynicism, which alternates without any apparent reason. One may appear mean and mad one day, and sweet and jovial the next day. Still other signs include a deterioration of physical appearance, an attitude of sullen withdrawal, being less tolerant of criticism or advice, becoming one tracked, mentally focusing on one thing for hours, and losing all sense of humor.[15]

Rediger declares that after seeing and counseling many pastors who are burned out, he is able describe what the

burnout syndrome looks like in pastors. Rediger describes
the appearance of burned out pastors as:

- *Physically. Low energy. Weight change. Exhausted
  appearance. Significant change in sleep patterns.
  Motor difficulties such as lack of coordination,
  tremors, twitches. Frequent headaches and gastric
  upset. Loss of sexual vigor. Hypochondriacal
  complaints.*

- *Emotionally. Apathy. One-track mind and loss of
  creativity. Paranoid obsessions. Constant irritability.
  Constant worrying. Loss of humor or development of
  gallows humor. Sporadic efforts to act as if everything
  is back to normal. Complaints of loneliness. Inability
  to be playful or become interested in diversionary
  activities. Excessive crying. Random thought patterns
  and inability to concentrate. Hopelessness.*

- *Spiritually. Significant changes in moral behavior.
  Drastic changes in theological statements. Loss of
  prayer and meditational disciplines. Development
  of moral judgmentalism. Loss of faith in God and
  themselves. One-track preaching and teaching. Listless
  and perfunctory performance of clergy-role duties.
  Loss of joy and celebration in spiritual endeavors.
  Cynicism.*[16]

These characteristics, as Rediger suggests, are seldom all seen in one person, but the burned out person will exemplify a combination of two or more from each of the categories. Having some of these characteristics does not necessarily indicate burnout, because persons who are discouraged, tired, or even bored may indicate these, but it is the combination of these characteristics with depth and pervasiveness that signals burnout. Burnout is the exhaustion of resources, not just being tired, discouraged, or cynical.[17]

BURNOUT: BIBLICAL EXAMPLES

The Bible is full of real life examples of success and faithfulness for the modern day pastor to follow. It is also replete with examples of failure, despair, disillusionment, and exhaustion (burnout). All together, the Bible reveals the full range of human reality even within biblical persons who are acclaimed today.

A glimpse of exhaustive sacrifice is found in Philippians chapter two. In this chapter, Paul encourages the saints at Philippi to receive with gladness a fellow companion of his, and laborer for the Lord, named Epaphroditus. Epaphroditus ministered to Paul, and worked alongside Paul. According to *Philippians 2:29, 30*, Paul told them to receive him therefore in the Lord with all gladness, and hold such men in esteem; because for the work of Christ he came close to death, not regarding his life, to supply what was lacking in your service toward me.[18] He was near death because of the work of the ministry. Without all of the details about Paul's faithful companion Epaphroditus, I can only say that he did not regard his own life for the sake of the ministry.

This Epaphroditus fact is all too true. Many in ministry, particularly pastoral ministry, either disregard the signs of exhaustion, whether physical, spiritual, or emotional, or they do not recognize the need to pace themselves. Pastors who allow themselves to be treated and placed on the pedestal as though they never tire and are always available are susceptible to experience non-fulfillment and lack of meaning in their ministry. Succumbing to the phrase and question by one parishioner that "pastors should not burnout,"... and "how can they burn out?" only leads to a denial of the fact that pastors do burn out and experience its effect upon their lives. The more I reflected on this statement, the more I

> *Many in ministry, particularly pastoral ministry, either disregard the signs of exhaustion, whether physical, spiritual, or emotional, or they do not recognize the need to pace themselves.*

felt as though the parishioner believed the level of spiritual yearning, emotional need, and physical balance for a pastor was altogether different from his. "Ministers are human too," and the truth is that many who enter ministry are very needy people. This does not mean that those in ministry should not be ministers, but it does mean that they should be honest about their needs or they will end up in trouble.[19]

Jody Seymour, in her book <u>A Time for Healing: Overcoming the Perils of Ministry</u>, points out in a study of the ministerial personality, the reality of the neediness of persons in ministry. It showed that "ministers tended to be more guilt-ridden, anxious, self-punishing in the face of hostility and aggression, more insecure, defensive, passive, conforming, dependent, rebellious, and idealistic than other people."[20] To understand ministerial humanity is to understand that pastors feel pain, experience major setbacks, and can indeed burn out. It must be stated that just because clergy people are God's people they are not exempt from the stresses that other humanitarian people experience.[21]

"Look at Jeremiah! Even though Jeremiah knew that he had been chosen by God, he did not try to hide from God, but he shared his very human struggles with God."[22] Jeremiah is a prime example of a man of whom the zeal of the Lord consumed and yet, Jeremiah is a prime example of clergy burnout. In ministry, affirmation often provides the adrenaline needed to continue on. When the very ones we serve do not give back that affirmation or feedback we need, sadness occurs. How often has a minister heard "you are paid to do it!"[23] Jeremiah's way of sharing this exasperation is found in *Jeremiah 18:20.*

> *In ministry, affirmation often provides the adrenaline needed to continue on.*

> *Should good be repaid with evil?*
> *Yet they have dug a pit for me.*
> *Remember that I stood before you*
> *and spoke in their behalf*
> *to turn your wrath away from them.*

Jeremiah, like so many ordained pastors had the need and desire to be liked and accepted. Even when his prophetic word was harsh and judgmental, he hoped that he would still be liked and well received. This need to be stroked, combined with the fire of the Lord's Word was a rough combination for Jeremiah. It was a combination destined for pastoral burnout. Jeremiah's burnout experience can be found in *Jeremiah 20:7, 14,* and *18.*

O Lord, thou hast deceived me,
and I was deceived;
thou art stronger than I,
and thou hast prevailed....
Cursed be the day
On which I was born!
The day when my mother bore me,
let it not be blessed!...
Why did I come forth from the womb
to see toil and sorrow,
and spend my days in shame?[24]

Jeremiah exemplifies the loneliness that comes in the journey of ministry that many possibly experience. He says in chapter 15:17-18

I did not sit in the company of merrymakers,
nor did I rejoice;
I sat alone, because thy hand was upon me,
for thou hadst filled me with indignation.
Why is my pain unceasing,
My wound incurable,
Refusing to be healed?
Wilt thou be to me like a deceitful brook,
Like waters that fail?[25]

This is a description of a tired clergy person who does not want to go on anymore. Like Jeremiah, there are times when clergy find themselves dropped into "empty cisterns." "Ministry takes us along paths where there are empty, waiting pits. Sometimes we get dropped in, and sometimes we simply fall in."[26] All clergy in ministry need to admit that there are times when we need to get a break and seek help. Pretending that we do not need help from others is disingenuous.[27] Another biblical example of burnout can be seen in the life of Elijah. In *I Kings* chapters 18 and 19, Elijah is victorious over the priests of Baal on Mount Carmel, and his own prayers bring about the end of the drought. This "defeat was so total that it sent Elijah retreating into the wilderness disheartened and bewildered, for Queen Jezebel, enraged at Elijah's destruction of her priests, hounded him unmercifully, renewed her persecution of Yahweh, and drove Elijah out of the land of Israel, into an isolated and homeless refugee."[28] Alone and in the desert, Elijah becomes so greatly depressed and discouraged that he wishes he were dead. He even asks the Lord, to take his life. Elijah, in this state gives us a prime example of burnout in pastoral (prophetic) ministry. Elijah gave his all, and in spite of his best efforts, he apparently feels like he has lost everything. He only wants to die, because he feels like a failure.

However, the Lord does not respond to Elijah's sense of despair and failure. He does not see as Elijah sees. His thoughts are not Elijah's thoughts, and His ways are not like Elijah's ways.[29] But the Lord does send an angel to feed and lift Elijah to send him on his way towards Mount Sinai. Once on Mount Sinai, Elijah winds up in a cave, still discouraged, waiting on a manifested sign from God. When the Lord shows up, He asks Elijah what was he doing in the cave. Elijah begins to dialogue with the God of heaven about how he failed the Lord, and how he alone survived the slaughter of Jezebel. Then he describes to the Lord that he is the only true prophet left. The Lord assures Elijah that he will be with him, and asks Elijah to return to anoint a new people and royalty to replace the leadership of Ahab and Jezebel. The Lord also informs Elijah that everyone is not dead. He tells Elijah that there are seven thousand people who have not bowed down or kissed Baal's idols. Elijah, with his heart encouraged and renewed, overcomes his sense of failure and returns to Israel to complete the work of the Lord.[30] Elijah represents pastors who started their ministry with boldness and great zeal, only to experience perceived failure

> *Elijah represents pastors who started their ministry with boldness and great zeal, only to experience perceived failure and exhaustion.*

and exhaustion. He also represents those who leave pastoral ministry burned out, only to return again.

RENEWAL DEFINED

In <u>Funk and Wagnalls Collegiate Dictionary</u>, renewal is defined as "the act of renewing, or the state of being renewed." Renew is defined as "to make new or as if new again, or to restore to a former or sound condition."[31] For the sake of this work, renewal will be referred to as establishing a new beginning. To begin again, Adventist pastors should not overlook the great necessity of living a holistic life. It is a fact that Adventists emphasize healthy living and teach that pure air, sunlight, abstemiousness, proper rest, moderate exercise, proper diet, the use of water, and trust in divine power are essential.[32] However, even though Adventist pastors counsel others about properly caring for their physical, spiritual, and emotional health, some tend to live as though these laws do not apply to them and that they are immune to the repercussions if not obeyed. Could it be, that Adventist pastors believe the Lord's work will shield them from the natural laws that affect everyone else?

As a prescription for renewal from burnout, or even better, as a precaution or prevention of burnout,

Adventist ministers should pay careful attention to their health (mind, body, and soul). They should strive to live a balanced life spiritually, physically, and emotionally. The personal practice of a regular prayer life and bible study, will help to maintain a deep spiritual connection with God. Physical exercise, eating properly and avoiding cholesterol that is so hazardous to ministerial health, and getting sufficient rest are essential in the area of prevention and renewal. Adventist pastors should also practice forgiveness, knowing that perpetual anger is not good for the their psyche or soul. Laughing and enjoying life, taking vacations and practicing stress-reducing methods are also essential in maintaining a merry heart that is medicinal. Renewal is a process that honors God. Servant ministry requires us to be vessels fit for service. Either we will be good for something, or good for nothing. Therefore it is super essential that our devotion towards living a balanced life is practiced passionately, thus enabling us to better carry out the task of ministry.[33]

The fact that clergy burnout has been widely written about, clarifies its legitimacy and prevalence as an issue of

> *The personal practice of a regular prayer life and bible study, will help to maintain a deep spiritual connection with God.*

study among concerned pastors and caregivers. However, because of the limited research among Adventist pastors, I desire to shed light on the subject. Therefore, this book represents my concerns as a pastor, and attempts to address the issue of pastoral burnout and renewal in the Seventh-day Adventist pastoral ministry. By implementing research, it seeks to access causes of pastoral burnout. Through personal integration it seeks to define and elaborate what it means to be an Adventist pastor. Furthermore, it is my hope that through this work, Adventist pastors will be made aware that burnout in ministry can be prevented. Moreover, it is my hope that pastors who have left pastoral ministry because they were burned out will find resources in this book to re-enter pastoral ministry renewed, revitalized, and able to use it as a resource for their rejuvenation.

CHAPTER 2

FLAME EXTINGUISHERS IN MINISTRY
Causes of Pastoral Burnout

"Out of affliction's dark comes
spiritual light."

— John Bunyan —

Come to Me, all you who labor and are heavy laden, and I will give you rest. Take My yoke upon you and learn from Me, for I am gentle and lowly in heart, and you will find rest for your souls. For My yoke is easy and My burden is light.

Matthew 11:28-30 NKJV

FLAME EXTINGUISHERS IN MINISTRY
Causes of Pastoral Burnout

Defend my cause and redeem me;
preserve my life according to your promise.

Psalm 119:154

What causes burnout? Sources of burnout in ministry are many and varied. However, in pastoral ministry, a lack of positive feedback can be predictive of burnout. Conflicting role demands and the ambiguity regarding pastors jobs, expectations about the pastorate and personal achievement, unrealistic or unmet goals, the loss of ideological commitment, a lack of affirmation or positive feedback, job overload, being over burdened with the trivial and unimportant, and the loss of moral purpose has all been linked to pastoral burnout. Personal views and expectations in ministry can be a source of burnout; and even pastors motivation and personality, including low self esteem, the inability to set limits, the lack of assertiveness, a strong need to have the approval of others, can also be seen as sources of burnout.

Organizational sources of burnout may include a constant unfinished workload at church, bureaucracy in institutional churches (churches typically on college campuses), the lack of feedback (not knowing if you are being effective or not), and, of course the pressures that come with ministry. Interpersonal sources of burnout may result from long-term member counseling, strained working relations with other pastors and conference administrators, and even relations with family and friends. It has been noticed that the higher the member involvement with the pastor or the greater the contact with members as it relates to care giving, such as an increase in counseling sessions or in conflict caseloads, or a greater percentage of time spent settling differences, the greater the possibility of burnout.[1]

Jody Seymour declares that much of the pain pastors experience in ministry is caused by their unwillingness or inability to face their own human interpersonal needs.

Jody Seymour declares that much of the pain pastors experience in ministry is caused by their unwillingness or inability to face their own human interpersonal needs. She says:

Somehow ministers think that they can skip over these needs and go on to help others. But it only takes a brief look at psychological dynamics to see the danger involved in overlooking personal needs. The neglected human need of the minister is transferred onto the persons and congregations who are being served. Combine this with the transference that occurs in the other direction, from the congregation and individual church members towards the minister, and the result is either ego inflation or weariness.[2]

This transference can feel good to the pastor at first, but these feel-good strokes can quickly turn to weariness.[3] John Sanford writing about transference says:

At first when we carry a transference for people it seems desirable because it is flattering, but sooner or later we experience it as a burden and it begins to tire us. For one thing, to carry transference means that something has been handed to us that we are expected to live up to. It also means that if our all-too-human reality should break through and disrupt the transference, the person will see us in terms of a negative transference for someone. Most of all, it wearies us to carry a transference because we are essentially carrying some of the psyche of other people that they need to find within themselves.[4]

Therefore, because of the load clergy people carry, it is essential that they have someone with whom they can turn, and whom they can be real with. It is essential that ministers have someone to talk to in order that they might maintain a personal sense of reality and the energy to continue ministry.[5] Thus, the causes of burnout in ministry will be viewed through the ambiguity of pastors job descriptions, the dilemmas of finding balance with church hierarchy, personal and family life, the misunderstandings of their roles, unrealistic expectations, and relational conflict.

CLARITY OF THE JOB

Burnout occurs when pastors misunderstand their job description. Many pastors consider preaching to be their chief function; the laity would also agree. It has been said that preaching "covers a multitude of sins." While not to minimize the importance of good and strong biblical preaching in the Adventist church, the teaching or equipping role of the pastor should take more time and precedence than the preaching role. This role is out of harmony with the biblical understanding that defines who a pastor is. The primary job is to teach and equip others to join them in ministry as co-laborers with God. Yet most pastors practice the opposite. They spend far more time preparing and preaching sermons than they do teaching members how to perform their ministry.[6] Ministers should spend more time teaching and educating than they do preaching. They should teach members how to give to others the same knowledge of the Word that they have received.[7]

> *The teaching or equipping role of the pastor should take more time and precedence than the preaching role.*

It has been my experience that many Adventist pastors fail to follow this counsel. In many churches the work would not get done, if the pastors did not do it.[8] This should not be! For too long have perfectionist, compulsive, and workaholic pastors done most of the work. Pastors have done themselves an injustice, and God a dis-service by not involving and equipping the laity in ministry. God does not require that we keep giving milk to our congregations; He desires that they grow up to eat the meat of the Word. Pastors who do most of the work without delegating or training the membership how to work will eventually work themselves to exhaustion. Listen to the words of

Jethro as he spoke to his son-in-law Moses in *Exodus 18:13-26* regarding the necessity of delegation for Moses' longevity.

> *The next day Moses took his seat to serve as judge for the people, and they stood around him from morning till evening. When his father-in-law saw all that Moses was doing for the people, he said, "What is this you are doing for the people? Why do you alone sit as judge, while all these people stand around you from morning till evening?"*
>
> *Moses answered him, "Because the people come to me to seek God's will. Whenever they have a dispute, it is brought to me, and I decide between the parties and inform them of God's decrees and laws."*
>
> *Moses' father-in-law replied, "What you are doing is not good. You and these people who come to you will only wear yourselves out. The work is too heavy for you; you cannot handle it alone. Listen now to me and I will give you some advice, and may God be with you. You must represent the people before God and bring their disputes to Him. Teach them the decrees*

and laws, and show them the way to live and the duties they are to perform. But select capable men from all the people–men who fear God, trustworthy men who hate dishonest gain–and appoint them as officials over thousands, hundreds, fifties and tens. Have them serve as judges for the people at all times, but have them bring every difficult case to you; the simple cases they can decide themselves. That will make your load lighter, because they will share it with you. If you do this and God so commands, you will be able to stand the strain, and all these people will go home satisfied."

Moses listened to his father-in-law and did everything he said. He chose capable men from all Israel and made them leaders of the people, officials over thousands, hundreds, fifties and tens. They served as judges for the people at all times. The difficult cases they brought to Moses, but the simple ones they decided themselves.

Duplication is God's method for his work to be completed through us, by Him. Through the training of pastors, ministers, and ministries, God's work is duplicated and the "Good News" is spread all over the world.

This issue is addressed in the book Gospel Workers, page 196, where it states, "in laboring where there are already some in the faith, the minister should at first seek not so much to convert unbelievers, as to train the church members for acceptable co-operation."[9] In other words, the author is saying that the first job of a minister is to train his/her members before even reaching out in soul winning.

The question may arise, why is this so important? It is important because whenever the pastor "takes over the ministry function of the church and neglects the training function, the church becomes weak spiritually,"[10] and the church depends on the pastor for most of the ministry that they too, should be able to provide. Training and teaching allow the pastor to marshal the membership with his vision instead of being marshaled by the membership. This will add to the length, breadth, and height of the pastoral sojourn.

> Whenever the pastor "takes over the ministry function of the church and neglects the training function, the church becomes weak spiritually."

I agrees with Russell Burrill in seeing a definite connection between how a pastor governs the church and the spirituality of the congregation. He believes that pastors who spend the bulk of their time ministering to members will foster a weak church spiritually.[11] I would add that the pastor would also become weak. Burrill states, that the pastors who spend the bulk of their time training and equipping the membership for service will have a much stronger church spiritually.[11] As the church grows in service, so they will grow spiritually. There is something about serving others and opening the Bible with others that takes the mind off personal problems. Service teaches the eternal principle of giving. Giving when practiced helps to develop a sense of dependence on God. This is essential in the growth of a spiritually strong church, because it becomes less dependent on the pastor and more dependent on God.

One pastor desired to start a male chorus. It was a great idea, but it was not received well because the pastor was the one who was starting the singing group. It was felt that the growth of the group would be stunted because everyone would look to the pastor for direction, whether present or absent. In other words, the members perceived greater ownership and investment by them starting the ministry, which would lead to a longer commitment because they would have ownership. Testimonies for the Church, Volume 7, supports the right directive for the minister. Pastors should not spend the bulk of their time straightening out the church, as much as they should be practicing the work of the church. There will always be work in the Church, and attention will always need to be given in the church, but members that are constantly looked after and labored for, become religious weaklings. If most of the effort that has been put forth for those who know the truth had been put forth for those who have never heard the truth, how much further would the gospel be advanced?[13] "Nurture for the sake of nurture produces spiritual weaklings."[14]

The potential for pastoral burnout can be great when the Adventist pastor does not train the membership to do the work of the ministry and perceives unrealistically or inappropriately through mission and evangelism that they should give most of the Bible studies, lead in evangelistic meetings, participate in all outreach activities, foster church nurture, and lead out administratively.

FINDING BALANCE – A DILEMMA

The inability of pastors to find a balance in relationship to church hierarchy, personal life, and family life causes burnout. Dilemmas come when the pastor is unable to find a balance between meeting the objectives of the upper organizations (i.e., the conferences) and meeting the needs of the congregation. This inability to find balance may disrupt the

> *The inability of pastors to find a balance in relationship to church hierarchy, personal life, and family life causes burnout.*

focus of specific church needs and goals, and may even cloud the implementation of church priorities for its particular community. Finding balance between the Adventist world church needs and vision, and the priorities of the local church, is one that the Adventist pastor needs to be able to accomplish. Finding this balance between local church and conference needs causes dilemmas in which Adventist pastors often find themselves inextricably woven. Leading a congregation in the twenty-first century requires a spiritual arsenal full of total dependence upon the Holy Spirit and complex skill training, as well as emotional and physical stamina. Stress and dilemmas are a normal part of the ministerial journey. Pastoral dilemmas are definitely a part of contemporary ministry. Webster's Dictionary defines dilemma as "a choice or a situation involving choice between equally unsatisfactory alternatives, and a difficult or persistent problem."[15]

The Adventist pastor that stays in general harmony with the congregation, and in purposeful agreement with the denominational value system and its theology, as well as, remaining in touch with the community needs where the church resides will function very well as minister of the gospel. The mere mention of harmony suggests that "the church shares many of the same human tensions and demands as any other human institution."[16] Yet because of the peculiar nature of the church and the work it poses, there remain some peculiar dilemmas.

For instance, in the Seventh-day Adventist Church, most of the major mission emphasis and strategic policies that affect pastoral ministry all come from the church divisional level. Employment, pastoral moves, retirement, and major evangelism funding are handled on the local conference level. In addition, most of the full-time pastors are paid on a similar wage scale, no matter the church size or level of responsibility. There may, however, be slight differences in the mileage pay, cost of living allowance, and working percentage. This too is an example of implementation from the upper divisions down to the local church. The General Conference, which is the world headquarters for the Seventh-day Adventist Church, is located in Silver Spring, Maryland. The Adventist Church is structured in Divisions, Unions, Conferences, and local churches. Because the Seventh-day Adventist Church is such a large worldwide church, structured in territorial fields around the world, pastors in congregations may feel that their voices are not heard.

Another dilemma arises when pastors choose to remain true to God's word amidst differing popular opinion. This conviction, at times, clashes against the denomination, congregation, community, home life, and even personal desire. This clash of convictions can add stressful dilemmas to the work of the pastor, which if it occurs repeatedly, may potentially lead to burnout. The criteria for determining whether a conviction should be held or not, is usually based on their personal understanding of God's moral revelation and will for their lives. This is understood in a great way through "the calling."

William H. Willimon, in his book <u>Clergy and Laity Burnout</u>, suggests that "we may disagree with our church hierarchy, adjudication, or polity on certain matters. It is fair to fight within the family," he says. "But when no one feels any longer that he or she is a part of the family, that is a different matter. Pastors and laity must feel that, while they may quibble with this or that denominational program or leader, they are still part of the denomination and are in sympathy with its general direction.

Pastors and laity must feel that, while they may quibble with this or that denominational program or leader, they are still part of the denomination and are in sympathy with its general direction.

Denominational change in direction or personality and change in the personality of the pastor or layperson can lead to a serious break between the individual and the institution."[17]

The relationship between the Adventist pastor and the hierarchical organization is one that must be understood in order to find balance. It is a fact in the Seventh-day Adventist ministry that "conferences depend almost totally on pastors for church growth and nurture. Conference money comes from churches. The income of the conference depends on the ministry of its pastors,"[18] and "through the actions of the conference executive committee (a territorial governing body), administrators provide significant financial security to their ministers. Unlike many clergy, Adventist pastors do not have to raise their own wages. Salaries may not always seem generous, but they are almost always dependable."[19] Even though some view the joining of any organization as placing limitations on their freedom, Adventist pastors are free to accept church employment, and understand that by doing so, they accept with that employment, full responsibilities of their particular pastoral ministry. The Seventh-day Adventist Minister's Manual suggests that by accepting employment ministers obligate themselves to trust their leaders, by cherishing the spirit of confidence. They are to support their leaders even when they differ, as long as it is not contrary to their own conscience. They need to consult their leaders, and hold their leaders accountable. Employment encourages Adventist pastors to "think freely, but to speak loyally."[20]

The concept of "finding a balance" to avoid dilemmas in working relationships as a pastor within the Adventist ministry is by no means new. It is a shaper of identity and the process of tension in personal integration. This dilemma is forged between our personal identity and our professional life. Congregations must be educated on this existing relationship between the pastors

> *God calls pastors long before they are hired or even recognized by the "bretheren".*

professional lives and their personal identities. God calls pastors long before they are hired or even recognized by the "bretheren". So the paycheck is not the source for diligence, but rather a temporary reward. The Seventh-day Adventist Encyclopedia, reveals

> *the SDA form of church government came to have characteristics of several systems particularly the Congregational, with its emphasis on local church authority; the Presbyterian, which provides for government by elected representatives; and in some points the Methodist, in that it has conferences as organizational units and in that the conference assigns ministers to the local churches. However, these features were not conscious imitations but grew out of the situations and needs of the developing SDA groups.*[21]

The Adventist Church was organized as a system, government, or polity to direct "the affairs of the church in an orderly manner. Organization functions to preserve the identity of a church society, to maintain purity of doctrine, to discipline members, to direct concerted efforts, and to care for the temporal as well as the spiritual existence of the church."[22] It is essential that Adventist pastors understand the church organization in which they accept employment. Finding balance in their professional relationships with the church hierarchy, congregation, community, and home life is vital in the life long relationship of a call to ministry.

BALANCE WITH CHURCH HIERARCHY

Inappropriate balance in the relationship with the church hierarchy can cause burnout for pastors. The potential for burnout arises in Adventist ministry in relationship to the pastor and conference when first, pastors feel as if the conference (denominational authority) does not support them, especially as it relates to the ministry in the local congregation. It is easy to sense a lack of support in ministry; to feel as though you are on a deserted island. When pastors feel that the conference brethren will only listen to their members in an instance of conflict, and act on their word without confirmation, it tends to isolate the pastor even more. This causes a great dilemma in the life of the pastor. The potential for burnout also arises when the dilemma to support the conference and its programs overrides the local church and its programs, especially as it evolves around finances.

It is true that goals do clash in a conference system when the financial needs of the local church are diluted because of conference wide initiatives. This is particularly true if a church has a large mortgage loan on the church property. While most of the funds received by a local conference are through church tithes, mission offerings, and conference initiatives in the Adventist Church, they are distributed for ministry through salary, mission, organization etc., and while these are all necessary and very legitimate, it leaves the local pastors with tough decisions to make in support of the agreed relationship. These decisions at times are real dilemmas for the pastors of congregations.

It must be clear that I am not an advocate of the Congregationalist church approach to ministry in the Adventist Church, by which I mean a totally autonomous and self-governing church, detached from any hierarchy. That system also has its weaknesses. However, even with possible dilemmas and clashes the Adventist pastor shares many positives in the relationship with the hierarchy of the church. One is that in this relationship between the hierarchical organization and the local church, the denominational headquarter executives tend mostly to be ministers who usually have many years of pastoral experience. The parish ministry, therefore, shapes their mindset. And many in these positions are called to design programs that assist in ministry to help pastors train members for ministry on the local church level. The key person of contact in this relationship between conference and congregation is the pastor. But depending on the relationship and morale, they may see these headquarters-initiated programs as just one more standard to which they must measure up.[23] So when the needs of the local congregation clash with conference goals it can create a stressful scenario.

BALANCE IN PERSONAL LIFE

Inappropriate balance in pastors personal lives will cause burnout. Pastoral dilemmas are usually the most exhausting when they occur in the personal life and family life of the minister. Dilemmas may arise in their personal lives when what they preach does not match up with what they practice. Dilemmas occur in pastors family lives because of this contradiction of lifestyle, but even more, they occur when the job, or church life, is woven together and becomes one with family time and home life.

Dilemmas usually rear their heads in the personal life of ministers when they cease to be honest with themselves. Lying is not only contradictory; it kills the repentant

> *Be who you say you are, and be what you teach.*

spirit. Chasing their own words to make full proof of them, will wear out pastors. In other words, be who you say you are, and be what you teach. Pastors should practice heeding the words of Paul to Titus in chapter 2:7-8: In everything set them an example by doing what is good. In your teaching show integrity, seriousness and soundness of speech that cannot be condemned, so that those who oppose you may be ashamed because they have nothing bad to say about us.

> *Jesus' teaching was so effective because He was what He taught. As preachers, we must be what we ask others to be, believe what we expect them to believe, and love Christ the way we want them to love.*
>
> *The ministry, perhaps more than any other profession, presumes that your vocation and your personal life are inseparable. In choosing a surgeon or a mechanic, you probably want competence more than you want character. Not so with ministers. What we are as people takes precedence over what we do as ministers.*[24]

◆

What we are as people takes precedence over what we do as ministers.

◆

In order to prevent the dilemmas that pastors cause themselves in relationship to the conference, church, community, and home, pastors must practice honesty, integrity, forgiveness, and righteousness. The pastor must practice this or ministry will become a façade on the stress wheel of life.

BALANCE IN FAMILY LIFE

Inappropriate balance in pastors home lives, as it relates to their job or church life, will lead to burnout. Finding this balance requires heavenly wisdom and much prayer. It also requires a systematic plan to cherish and protect their homes. In the family, dilemmas arise when home life is constantly intruded upon by the work of the church. Work in the ministry often bleeds over into the home, and unless it is deliberately monitored, it will be the cause of great stress in their lives. Family life in the home is tugged upon through unfinished church business for meetings, missed appointments at home and church, being misunderstood, the telephone, the answering machine, being guilty, feeling guilty, anger, parenthood,

> *In the family, dilemmas arise when home life is constantly intruded upon by the work of the church.*

frustration, the next emergency, and being a husband or wife, father or mother. Whatever the case, all at some time in ministry either accompany the pastor home, or are waiting at home for the pastor to arrive. It has been my experience and belief that the home, where the family resides, should be a place of refuge. It should be a castle of peace, but lest the Adventist pastor misunderstand me, they should know that "traditionally, pastors families experience special stresses, and historically, the family has been neglected."[25] Think about the apostles, if they had spouses and families, they seemed not to give any special attention to them. Paul, it could be said, was married at one time, but chose to emphasize the benefits of ministering single. Seventh-day Adventists have roots in Methodism. Its founder, John Wesley did not marry until he was 48 years old. Even then, he chose to cut his honeymoon short because he felt as though being married should not hinder him any more than if he was single. This still does not excuse the neglect of the family. Even Jesus was oriented to his family, and especially his mother. The apostles probably did not have normal family relationships because of their confinement to the distinctiveness of itinerate missionary journeys.[26]

In the Bible however, the model for the pastor in relationship to the family is seen in the family centered counsel of Paul to the bishop in *1 Timothy 3:2-5*.

Now the overseer must be above reproach, the husband of but one wife, temperate, self-controlled, respectable, hospitable, able to teach, not given to drunkenness, not violent but gentle, not quarrelsome, not a lover of money. He must manage his own family well and see that his children obey him with proper respect. (If anyone does not know how to manage his own family, how can he take care of God's church?)

Because pastors experience stress, because pastoral spouses experience stress, and because their children experience stress, the first and foremost ministry of pastors must be to the family. "Maintaining a happy, exemplary family has enough problems, that make it challenging, but it is well worth the effort. If something goes wrong, do not settle for the burial of family relationships gone dead. Be Christian about and seek a resurrection. It will bless your family and multiply the effectiveness of your ministry."[27] Though friend or foe is the cause of serious home dilemmas, pastors, should practice being deliberate and determined to dedicate quality time with their families regularly. As pastors live Godly, and strive to be the greatest Dad or Mom or Spouse this world has ever known, their families will see Jesus' love coming, when they come home. Pastors should give time that their families can count on. They must give time around the house for chores, communicate intensely and sincerely with their children and spouses, affirm and confirm their family's importance. Lastly, seek the face of God daily with your family in prayer and devotion.[28] These steps and others, presented in chapter 4, will help the Adventist pastor confront the dilemmas in the family and prevent the burnout syndrome from occurring in the home.

Young pastors still in training, tend to imitate styles of ministry that have impacted them most. Therefore, it is only through personal experience and prayerful reasoning that ministry dilemmas can be tempered or screened.[29] "A student in preaching class, having experienced a ministry enamored with the prophetic teaching of the Old Testament, proclaimed the Word with all the thunder of a latter-day Amos. Moving beyond the duplication of what has been one's experience of ministry, to a personal style and understanding, is one of the most difficult tasks for aspiring ministers."[30] Especially when placed in dilemmas that

> *Moving beyond the duplication of what has been one's experience of ministry, to a personal style and understanding, is one of the most difficult tasks for aspiring ministers.*

confront personal convictions. Usually for the young minister, convictions are born or released in the heat of the battle or in the pressure of the "must decisions" needing to be made.

THE MISUNDERSTOOD ROLE OF THE PASTOR

Understanding the complex role of contemporary pastors gives insight into the necessity for spiritual connection, emotional care, and physical awareness. This is essential and important to life balance in the professional journey of Adventist pastors. Lloyd Rediger sees their role as all encompassing or engulfing. In fact, he sees their role as the only profession whereby their professional, personal, and religious faith are all wrapped up in a single package. "In other words," he says, "there is no escaping, except through anonymity."[31]

A former Adventist pastor, Dennis Wallstrom, received his Ph.D. from Fuller Theological Seminary. His dissertation entitled <u>Role Conflict and Burnout in the Ministry</u> researched 108 Adventist pastors' responses to role pressures that caused psychological strain in the Adventist ministry. Some of his findings included research in organizational psychology and the effects of role strain. He found, with some qualifications, that role-playing and role accommodation was shown to increase anxiety, reduce performance and commitment, and also increase the propensity to leave the ministry.[32]

Pastors seldom forget their role and expectations of their role. "People in other vocations can at least escape into their religious faith when the pressure is on."[33] But pastors must face the pressure with their work and faith wrapped altogether. Their call to ministry will always precede their response in declaration to the call.

> *Pastors must face the pressure with their work and faith wrapped altogether.*

Role as the vehicle…through which behaviors and expectations converge is a crucial concept for understanding the pressures upon the minister. The person who occupies a role is part of an ongoing cycle in which expectations from influential others are sent and received, responded to behaviorally, and then modified and communicated once again. Whatever their source, expectations of a minister's role take on a typically demanding and idealistic flavor.[34]

This is where calling and role collide to create certain dilemmas for the pastor. The strain on ministers to fulfill their expected roles often diminishes the initiation of God's call on the minister's life. Even pastor's spouses and children get caught in this role expectation which often is unrealistic and causes what Rediger terms "collateral vulnerability and collateral damage."[35]

"When a person marries a pastor or is intimately related to a pastor, the person is normally expected to take some interest in and to participate at some level in this role. The participation can vary from simply listening to the pastor talk about his experiences to becoming the unpaid assistant pastor. Even if a pastor's intimates (spouse, family, or close friends) can separate themselves from his role, the congregation and perhaps the denomination still will have at least some role-related expectations of them."[36]

If Adventist pastors do not have a clear understanding of their calling in relationship to their role and even employment, then misunderstandings, miscommunication, miscalculations, conflict, and stress will occur throughout their ministry. H. B. London, Jr. and Neil B. Wiseman, in their book <u>Your Pastor Is an Endangered Species</u>, describes this dilemma in everyday church life as the persistent struggle for pastors to find a meaningful existence amidst greater demands, low credibility, suspicious followers, and needy members.[37] Adventist pastors are often tugged between the hierarchical organizations (conference) desire, their personal convictions, unrealistic congregational expectations, community endeavors, and family needs. Reflecting and meditating on one's personal calling is a spiritual effort towards a new beginning.

UNREALISTIC EXPECTATIONS

Unrealistic expectations are detrimental to pastoral ministry. Unrealistic expectations generally cause diametrically opposing viewpoints that tend to create potentially fragile and volatile relationships between a minister and a congregation, and will cause burnout if the pastor tries to meet every expectation. The expectations between pastor and congregation vary. Essentially the problem revolves around what is expected of a pastor from the congregation, and what is expected of a congregation from a pastor. The pastor may be moving in the opposite direction of the congregation. They may have one idea, and the pastor another, and the conference authorities may have still another. The conflict over expectations

> *Unrealistic expectations are detrimental to pastoral ministry.*

centers around two needs. On the one hand, Adventist pastors need to be in charge of themselves and desire to live out their own identities in ministry. On the other hand, pastors need some tangible evidence of progress, of movement, of success, regardless of how it is measured. And furthermore, pastors that are called by God into the ministry, should be responsible to God. Yet, pastors must also answer the question, does God speak through the congregation and through the denominational hierarchy?[38]

Listen to the collision of confusing expectations from an ad written by a pulpit committee in a western state, recently published in a pastor's magazine: Seeking an exceptional, committed individual for unique ministry in central (name of site) willing to help us survive and reach our potential and be an active participant in maintaining a strong Christian witness with a stable congregation of 40 members, all ages. A national park is close, golf and fishing are convenient. Other recreational opportunities are within easy driving distance. Rock hounding paradise. This is a challenge. Prospective pastors must be willing to experience new perspectives, different culture, and great satisfaction. Tent-making or part-time position.[39]

As one thinks of the average pastor that reads this ad, maybe it could be perceived that this church is looking for a tent making pastor who can serve the church over 40 years, come what may. And who will help the church survive, fulfill their potential, and maintain a strong witness in the community. This ad would make you wonder whether or not Jesus would be hired to pastor there.[40] In contrast to what this ad implies, ministers do have considerations as to their most important priorities. A recent study revealed that pastors think a "fulfilling marriage, followed by the challenge of preaching, a sense of calling to the ministry, and satisfaction from pastoral care to be the most significant ministry enhancers. Yet these concerns apparently have low priority or perhaps no importance for the pastoral search committee who placed the ad seeking a pastor for this church of forty people. No wonder the church is experiencing confusion in so many places."[41]

H. B. London, Jr. and Neil B. Wiseman emphasize that serving as a pastor and serving as a lay leader in the church are vastly different positions. They suggest that pastors and lay leaders need to realize how enormously different they are and that neither will be able to fully understand or comprehend the other's perspective. In spite of encouraging signs that lay ministry is moving towards a great sense of the priesthood of believers – a wonderful revolution – there are still essential differences in intensity, academic and on-the-job training, insight and perspective, and viewpoint that must be accepted with love and grace.[42]

The pastor is faced with so many different expectations that they can never satisfy everyone. Pastors in the ministering roles can wear themselves completely out trying to satisfy all expectations. Pastors should not even try to fulfill every expectation or they will become exhausted, unfulfilled and anxious.[43] Many pastors work with ill-defined congregational expectations. And this causes them to feel as though they were always in a "no-win" situation. Expectations for their job performance are so diverse with no definite form, that relating to each individual parishioner's vague picture of what a "good pastor" looks like, will cause the poor pastor to never feel as though he or she is doing the job.[44]

One pastor described his dilemma as feeling as though

> *Pastors in the ministering roles can wear themselves completely out trying to satisfy all expectations.*

> *One pastor described his dilemma as feeling as though he had six hundred bosses with each of them having a different job description that they did not bother to show him.*

he had six hundred bosses with each of them having a different job description that they did not bother to show him. "Because of the ill defined nature of the pastoral ministry, the work demands a high level of internal control. Pastors probably have less peer supervision than any other profession. They are on their own. In conscientious persons, this encourages a heightened sense of responsibility, but it can lead to an oppressive situation if the person is not only conscientious but also a perfectionist and unrealistic."[45]

John Sanford suggests that the pastor and the Church governing body discuss the most important tasks for the minister. And even if they do not agree on the tasks, at least the matter is out in the open and discussed for understanding. John Sanford also suggests that a pastor set parameters by refusing to accept certain tasks, thereby eliminating an expectation that probably could not have been fulfilled anyway.[46]

Higher expectations are a living reality for the pastor.

Higher expectations are a living reality for the pastor. There can be no doubt that even in society there is a certain level of expectation in general, as it relates to the manner in which a pastor should talk, walk, and function as a minister. Admittedly, some of the recent scandal around clergy would have been passing chatter in other professions had it not been for the higher standards that society expects of ministers. This does not justify the inappropriate actions of some clergy, but simply to state the fact that there are higher expectations placed on those who are called to ministry. These expectations are not only within the community of faith, but also within the community at large.[47]

> *Society has expectations also concerning the ministry itself. Even in our post-Christian society, the church is viewed as an institution in society not unlike other organizations such as school, hospital, city hall and commercial firm. There is a certain public ownership, which gives public access when required. For instance, in many places a church wedding is still the norm. It is therefore expected that the church and services of clergy are readily available at the call even of those who never attend or support it. Refusal of either (church or clergy), for one reason or another, to be used for this purpose can and does evoke responses of hostility and anger. It is expected that the church and clergy will, upon request, participate in other rites of passage from christening to*

> *burial, community activities, public blessings and performances and broader social interaction out of duty with no compensation to either institution or person.*[48]

Society does have its expectations of clergy, and the expectations affect, whether internally or externally, the way in which pastors practice, perform, contribute, and serve. Particularly those that see the church as an institution to be swindled, whether it is a traveling bootleg preacher, or a wino off the street, they expect to gain sympathy in the form of money from the church through the pastor. When they are granted help or given money, it is usually done out of sympathy, compassion, or guilt. John Sanford who believes that the ministering person's proneness to guilt makes them vulnerable to manipulation, affirms this principle of service through guilt. He says:

> *clever people, including con artists, sense this weakness in the clergy person and can use it to make pastors their victim. They can even extract money from pastors if they prey on their fear of becoming guilty. As soon as a ministering person learns to deal with their guilt, all of this manipulation comes to an end. It is also guilt that makes it difficult for a ministering person to work effec-*

tively with potential suicides. Such people often do this because it will get them a lot of attention and not because they are serious about it. It enables them to control the ministering person, and they may intrude on his/her private life, call at all hours of the night and disturb his/her sleep, or make undue demands upon his/her working time. These kinds of cases that can cause exhaustion, mental stress, and loss of sleep over a prolonged period of time can be a threat to health. For some reason people assume that they have the right to intrude upon a ministering person even if they are not members of their congregation. It can get to the point that they even hate to hear the phone ring for fear of who may be calling with a demand that they will feel they must fulfill.[49]

Needless to say, if it gets to this point in pastors ministries, one's personal boundaries should be re-evaluated and re-drawn. Also pastors should use social professionals as referrals for solutions and intervention. This is an excellent way to receive help from those who may be much wiser and decisive, and from those who deal in crisis ministry everyday. The Adventist pastor should also involve the congregation in the process of the evaluation of needs, crisis, and emergencies. Pastors do not have to be in control of everything in the church because God did not make them omnipotent.[50] A committee could be designated, of which the pastor is not a part of, to handle the responsibility for interviewing the person or persons to access their needs. They could also be responsible for the designation and distribution of the church funds for those in crisis. This would alleviate and/or lighten the load of the community's expectation on the pastor solely.

Burnout is inevitable if the pastor tries to meet everyone's expectations.

Burnout is inevitable if the pastor tries to meet everyone's expectations.

Furthermore, one cannot be true to their convictions by attempting to meet everyone else's expectations. Pastors should know their limitations. They should not try to live up to all the expectations placed on them, by pretending to be "super human." Trying to meet all expectations is hypocritical and discouraging, because the pastor will never succeed. "Do not be misled by people who think you are ten feet tall and able to walk on water.

Trying to meet all expectations is hypocritical and discouraging, because the pastor will never succeed.

You cannot work a twenty-hour day and keep sweet. You cannot do everything everybody wants done. Besides, you are not supposed to."[51]

RELATIONAL CONFLICT

To provide meaningful ministry in the midst of unrealistic expectations is difficult, but to provide meaningful ministry under the tension of conflict is even more difficult and detrimental to ministers and their congregations. Many pastors have driven down burnout lane in the vehicle of relational conflict.

Charles Cosgrove and Dennis Hatfield define conflict in their book <u>Church Conflict</u> as "the expression (in words and actions) of disharmony between different opinions and desires present in all human systems."[52] "Conflict is sometimes overt, taking the form of an argument or even a (church fight). But often it remains hidden, manifesting itself in seemingly trivial ways…. And sometimes a seemingly petty open quarrel is really only a mask for a deeper and more serious quarrel beneath the surface."[53] Conflict is normal in the congregation, but it does not

> *Many pastors have driven down burnout lane in the vehicle of relational conflict.*

have to be accepted as the norm. Even though conflict is normal, coarseness, belligerence, and abuse in congregations do not have to be acceptable behavior for Christian congregations.[54]

Relational conflict arises in many ways in the church, and one of them is through the "Big T." Tradition in the church, as every pastor knows, can be an asset or foe. It can assist the pastor in transition between churches in a conference system of polity, or it can hinder the pastor in the congregational system. Tradition can blur the lines of biblical understanding, robe the church of its relevant historical perspective, or even narrow the church's understanding of ministry.[55]

Tradition is a way of saying or doing something, which comes from earlier times and has become identified not only with the past, but with how we view and understand ourselves today. Tradition may become altered or "tempered by time and the world with which it interfaces, but it continues as an expression of the uniqueness that gave it rise."[56]

"Each church within any denominational structure also functions with its unique and specific traditions. Such things as the position of the baptismal font, the covering on the communion table and what may properly be placed on the sacred furniture are unique to the local tradition and thinking of the congregation. Add this to the theological thinking of the congregation, which often is an eclectic mixture of teaching and cultural traditions," and that creates for the pastor the need to navigate through waters that may be uncharted.[57]

Therefore, denominational traditions, local congregational traditions, and personal traditions for the pastor must all be addressed, studied, and learned from. Some traditions may need to be encouraged, others forsaken, but none should hinder the process of spreading

Some traditions may need to be encouraged, others forsaken, but none should hinder the process of spreading the gospel, and none should be so revered as to take the place of God.

the gospel, and none should be so revered as to take the place of God. It needs to be stated in the recognition of potential burnout, that all these instances are woven in the fabric of stress over a period of time. They will thrive and venture from a molehill to a mountain.

Relational conflict may even arise in the community. Through dilemmas that confront the pastor like choosing whether or not to allow police to survey community rallies from the church roof top, knowing that they have on other occasions protected your church from graffiti; choosing to allow political groups to address issues at the church site, allowing politicians in the pulpit; etc. These are pastoral dilemmas that cause conflict in the local congregation of the Adventist church and require pastoral wisdom through conviction, discernment, and prayer.

Relational conflict that negatively affects pastors arises most frequently out of relationships between church members with other church members, pastors with members, members with pastors, and even pastors with other pastors. Conflict usually arises when congregational desires or preferences collide with pastoral convictions in areas of church administration, church operation, and biblical practice. For example, a pastor may be asked by church members to perform the wedding ceremony of a couple he/she has never seen before or counseled, from two different faith groups and insisting that the ceremony be held in the church. Another pastor may be faced with the political pressure of a demand that a member who is openly not living in harmony with biblical principles or teachings be allowed to serve as a church officer. Pastoral conflicts also arise when the role of mediation becomes a frequent occurrence. In other words, fre-

> *Conflict usually arises when congregational desires or preferences collide with pastoral convictions in areas of church administration, church operation, and biblical practice.*

quently serving as the go-between in emotional and passionate situations. Relational conflict has to do with cited differences that clash among personalities. They may clash over ideals, issues, or cherished convictions. Generally it is most likely that opposing people rather than opposing ideas will cause problems in church relationships. Relational conflict is inevitable and unavoidable in the church. As long as there are two individuals walking the same path, there will be differences that may or may not be possible to solve.

> *Relational conflict has to do with cited differences that clash among personalities.*

In ministry you must cope with criticism, complaints, and be able to negotiate through passionate subjects. You must be able to confront tough decisions and make controversial decisions. Handling family problems and dealing with clashes between traditionalists and visionaries, anthem singers and gospel music lovers, new members and lifetime members are all a part of the pastor's job. These issues occur daily in the life and relationships of the pastor and congregation. Conflict in

> *In ministry you must cope with criticism, complaints, and be able to negotiate through passionate subjects.*

the Adventist church comes through these and other variances in ministry.

In the Adventist church, relational conflict occurs during church officer elections, selection or placement of pastors, and during times when a conference, church, or pastor differ in church direction. Ultimately, every pastor will face or will have to address some form of conflict during their church pastorate. They will face some conflict that is not so major, and other conflicts that can become very time consuming.

When conflict is personally directed at the pastor, meaning the pastor's style, or the way meetings are conducted, or even at the pastor's family, it becomes an all consuming issue and has the potential to take a life of its own for the pastor. Conflict that is not properly addressed or dealt with by the Adventist pastor will affect relationships and leave stress, ulcers, and burnout in its wake for the pastor. Conflicts with members and conflicts between members flare up continuously. As stress analyst Hans Selye says, "the stress of living with one another still represents one of the greatest causes of distress."[58] My grandfather, a retired Adventist pastor, said it best when he declared "as long as you have two people on the planet you are going to have trouble."

Laity and pastors must face the fact that conflict is

almost inevitable whenever people serve together in groups. The Bible confirms this and solidifies that conflict started in the most truth filled center in the universe. It started in Heaven (Rev. 12:7-9). Conflict is also seen in scripture in many journeys of the patriarchs.[59] Some examples of biblical conflict will help shed light on conflict destruction, as well as being the impetus for restoration and healing.

Jacob and Esau

> *Genesis 27:41* states, Esau held a grudge against Jacob because of the blessing his father had given him. He said to himself, *"The days of mourning for my father are near; then I will kill my brother Jacob."*

Jacob and Esau were two brothers who were totally different from each other. Some would say they were opposites. Jacob's mother loved Jacob more than Esau, and Esau's father loved Esau more than he loved Jacob. The conflict centered on Jacobs's deception of his father and brother to receive the sacred blessing and birthright. Because he was the eldest, it rightly belonged to Esau. For years Esau carried the bitter taste of having been deceived, and even wanted to kill his brother, but through the matchless healer of time and divine intervention, these two brothers settled their differences according to Genesis 33:4-16.

Deception that causes conflict in ministry cannot always be settled over a short period of time; also one must recognize that mediation is not always a cure. I have discovered that there are times in ministry when conflict arises even among family members, and only through time and prayer can a solution be found.

> *Deception that causes conflict in ministry cannot always be settled over a short period of time.*

David and Saul

1 Samuel 18:5-9 states, Whatever Saul sent him to do, David did it so successfully that Saul gave him a high rank in the army. This pleased all the people, and Saul's officers as well.

When the men were returning home after David had killed the Philistine, the women came out from all the towns of Israel to meet King Saul with singing and dancing, with joyful songs and with tambourines and lutes. As they danced, they sang: "*Saul has slain his thousands, and David his tens of thousands.*"

Saul was very angry; this refrain galled him. "*They have credited David with tens of thousands,*" he thought, "*but me with only thousands. What more can he get but the kingdom?*" And from that time on Saul kept a jealous eye on David.

The relationship between Saul and David reveals tenuous conflict for years. Their conflict, or rather, Saul's conflict with David centered on Saul's insecurity and jealousy towards David. Insecurity and jealousy will always create conflict in relationships. Doubt not, under the yoke of jealousy and insecurity will come criticism. David never really understood why Saul grew to hate him; and that wounded him.

Hurt and anger are usually the by-products of unfair and unjustified criticism or jealousy. Pastors should remember while dealing with insecure leaders and jealous co-workers, that they can let go of those difficult relationships, they can protect themselves from negative people. They do not have to take the criticism that comes with conflict personally, and they do not have to remain angry.[60]

Paul and Barnabas

Acts 15:36-41 states, Some time later Paul said to Barnabas, *"Let us go back and visit the brothers in all the towns where we preached the word of the Lord and see how they are doing."* Barnabas wanted to take John, also called Mark, with them, but Paul did not think it wise to take him, because he had deserted them in Pamphylia and had not continued with them in the work. They had such a sharp disagreement that they parted company. Barnabas took Mark and sailed for Cyprus, but Paul chose Silas and left, commended by the brothers to the grace of the Lord. He went through Syria and Cilicia, strengthening the churches.

The conflict between Paul and Barnabas arose out of a disagreement whether or not to take someone on a missionary trip. Barnabas wanted John Mark to go with them, and Paul did not. Now these were two converted apostles, who had such heated contention over this issue that they each went their separate ways, with Barnabas taking John Mark. This gives us an example of agreeing to disagree. It has been my experience that this form of conflict management can be very effective over contentious issues. Paul and Barnabas obviously settled their differences because they can later be seen in ministry together in *Colossians 2:1, 9.*

Even these biblical examples of conflict were written in the past...to teach us, so that through endurance and the encouragement of the Scriptures we might have hope. *Romans 15:4.* There will be times in ministry when "reasonably unimportant issues, such as budgeting, carpet color, schedules for [Sabbath] services, music worship styles, choice of visiting preachers, and a thousand other small details manifest themselves on the pastor. Conflict may also arise when inappropriate behavior or unbecoming attitudes need to be challenged," but the pastor must always be careful not to appear condescending in these matters.[61] Even in the rejection of your own ministry by the ones you serve, pastors should make themselves available to offer the hope and healing of the gospel.[62]

> *Even in the rejection of your own ministry by the ones you serve, pastors should make themselves available to offer the hope and healing of the gospel.*

William E. Hulme, says in his book, <u>Managing Stress in Ministry</u> "that the congregation is like one big family, and like families, you will have dissension." He goes on to say that "churches as well as denominations repeatedly present a sad spectacle with their destructive interfamily feuding."[63]

The congregation is a convenient projection screen for all the individual frustrations its members experience outside the congregational community. Its organized structures are a tempting setting for the power plays and the control games so often blocked elsewhere by the impersonal structures of our society.

People who have unresolved problems with authority also find a convenient outlet in attacking the vulnerable authority of the clergy. Those who are really angry at God, for example, find a logical scapegoat in the pastor's symbolic role, because it is easier and safer to attack someone who is tangibly human than to attack the Ruler of the Universe.[64]

I believe that conflict left to itself will eventually destroy enthusiasm, which is so needed in the health and growth of the church. I also believe that if left alone, conflict will discourage members from inviting friends to worship services and will sap the efforts and energy from the pastor. Conflicts, in the words of one senior pastor, will keep you off guard and divert your attention.[65]

Conflicts that erupt in the congregation are stressful for the pastor, and if such conflicts are not managed well, polarizing factions can develop in which a "we versus they" mentality, can disrupt the community. Clergy can also fall into this alienating mood, categorizing the congregation as they. The imagery then is one of "over against" rather than of "along side of," and the dynamics of a win-or-lose power struggle are set in motion. Considering others in the conflict as opponents or adversaries aggravates the conflict.[66]

One pastor was surprised to notice that his members felt that they had to have a problem to talk to him and the healthy productive members

Pastors cease to be every members pastor when they choose to minister to a selected few.

all stayed away because they thought he was too busy.[67] This is because the church members noticed whom the pastor chose to spend most of his time with. Pastors cease to be every members pastor when they choose to minister to a selected few.

Members appreciate the pastor addressing problems and problem people in the church. They even appreciate the pastor spending time with members with frequent problems, but if the needy continue to dominate, valuable opportunities for building an active lay ministry may be lost; because proper time is even difficult to give to the faithful ministering lay person.[68] "The reality is that conflict is present and can be both useful and debilitating."[69] According to Lloyd Rediger, "the following generalizations can be made about our current conflict and ways of coping with it: conflict is real, persistent, and sometimes mean. Conflict can be normal, abnormal, or spiritual. Conflict can escalate into abuse and inflict collateral damage. Conflict can be managed poorly or well. Effective conflict management is not yet the norm in congregations or judicatories."[70]

> *The reality is that conflict is present and can be both useful and debilitating.*

The best choice for the pastor however, is to use conflict and to view conflict creatively to introduce positive possibilities. London and Wiseman suggest that, congregations and pastors should not place themselves in an emotional and administrative straitjacket by acting as if conflict and controversy do not exist.[71] Conflict really exists in congregational life, and it can be used creatively and even redemptively.[72] This will add to the effectiveness, longevity, and meaningful existence

> *Conflict really exists in congregational life, and it can be used creatively and even redemptively.*

in ministry. Otherwise "the alternative is to allow conflict to divide a church and scatter the flock."[73] Conflict can help to clarify issues, help potential solutions emerge, and provide a way to move toward a resolution of differences. Conflict can be useful as leaders confront each other honestly, consider each other's viewpoints, listen to each other's positions, and seek to make decisions that will unify the body of Christ.

Because there are so many stressors that open the door to burnout, the highly motivated Seventh-day Adventist pastor needs to be deliberate in maintaining a constant, personal and spiritual relationship with God. Periodic emotional self-care, and a consistent balance in physical life that includes proper diet, rest, and exercise must be observed. Otherwise burnout will creep in on them. Addressing pastoral burnout is extremely important to the life of the Adventist church, because burnout poses a serious problem to the wholeness, health, and existence of its leaders.

CHAPTER 3

IGNITING
What it means to be a Seventh-day Adventist Pastor

Now thank we all our God,
With heart and hands and voices,
Who wondrous things hath done in
whom His world rejoices.

— Catherine Winksorth —

Thanks be to God for his indescribable gift!

2 Corinthians 9:15 NIV

IGNITING

What it means to be a Seventh-day Adventist Pastor

*And this gospel of the kingdom will be preached
in the whole world as a testimony to all nations,
and then the end will come.*

Matthew 14:14

Seventh-day Adventist pastors, like most denominational pastors, have a unique history and a great heritage. The SDA pastor is an ordained or licensed minister. Ordained, meaning that they have received all rights and authorization to function and perform the duties of the pastoral office throughout the world church field. Licensed, meaning that they are functioning or serving as pastor on a tenured or trial basis until the conference deems they are to be ordained. In the Seventh-day Adventist Church titles like pastor and minister, are used interchangeably to mean the same thing, but the Seventh-day Adventist Encyclopedia gives distinction and additional credence to the pastor's responsibility and work under the title minister. A minister is "one authorized (by ordination) to conduct worship services, to preach, to perform the baptismal and marriage ceremonies, and to conduct the Lord's Supper."[1] In the Seventh-day Adventist usage of this term pastor, it means an ordained minister, or a licentiate, referring to a licensed minister. An SDA minister is addressed as Pastor or Elder—meaning an ordained minister only.[2]

Pastors are not considered to be regular office holders of the church and are not elected by the local church to hold the position of pastor. An ordained or licensed pastor is appointed by the conference or the mission committee, and is paid by the conference to do the work of the ministry in the church. The pastor's connection with the church organizationally is by appointment only, and may be changed by the conference or mission committee at any time.[3]

> Pastors are not considered to be regular office holders of the church and are not elected by the local church to hold the position of pastor.

The <u>Seventh-day Adventist Church Manual</u> states:

on assignment to a local church as pastor, the ordained minister ranks above the local elder or elders; these serve as his assistants. By virtue of his ordination to the ministry he is qualified to function in all church rites and ceremonies. He should be the spiritual leader and adviser of the church. He should instruct the church officers in their duties and plan with them for all lines of church work and activity.... the minister, with the assistance of the elders, is expected to plan for and lead out in all spiritual services of the church, such as Sabbath morning worship and prayer meeting, and should officiate at the communion service and baptism. He should not surround himself with any special body of counselors of his own choosing, but always work in cooperation with the duly elected officers of the church.[4]

From the onset of their clergy history, Seventh-day Adventist pastors have emphasized mission. Over the years, this has been expressed in action through evangelism, discipleship, and nurture. This chapter will argue that a distorted or inappropriate view of mission will lead an Adventist pastor to a feeling of underachievement or, worse, to a feeling that the task of ministry is unaccomplishable.

From the onset of their clergy history, Seventh-day Adventist pastors have emphasized mission.

HISTORICAL SEVENTH-DAY ADVENTIST DEFINITION OF PASTORAL MINISTRY

A Seventh-day Adventist pastor, whether ordained or licensed, serves in an assignment given by the conference to a church or district (more than one church), and is paid by that conference. They do not function as regular officers of the assigned church and their position cannot be elected. The pastor serves as the leader of the church and assists the church officers in carrying out their duties. Generally, they lead out in pulpit duties, chair the church board, and sit on committees for spiritual guidance and influence. It is a blessing that most churches have pastors in their churches or districts, because in the earlier years of the denomination churches did not have pastors. Traveling preachers or evangelists would visit infrequently, and the church had to function with the support of the local lay elder. [5]

Writing in 1883, W. H. Littlejohn, in his series on the Church Manual wrote in the Review and Herald, that the work of the SDA minister was largely evangelistic. Because of the shortage of pastors, "only enough attention was given to the older churches to keep them in good running order"[6] in the early years of the formal church.

For the SDA minister past and present, soul winning

is the first and great work to be accomplished. Those who work for God should first and foremost strive to introduce people to the Gospel of Jesus Christ. Their primary work should be to seek and to save the lost. This is their transcendent task. Nothing is to take the place of this; nothing is to divert their attention from this supreme objective. "To win souls to the kingdom of God must be the first consideration. With sorrow for sin and with patient love, they must work as Christ worked, putting forth determined, unceasing effort."[7]

But according to the Manual for Ministers in the Seventh-day Adventist Encyclopedia the responsibilities of the Adventist minister go even further. It suggests that the responsibility of the minister is two-fold. They are not only to make disciples, but also to teach disciples. Meaning that, as the new disciples are brought in and introduced to Christ, they are to also be built up in Christ. Pastors should not only be evangelists, but also shepherds of the flock. They should seek to be well balanced and well rounded ministers for the Lord. As great soul winners and great pastors, they will declare all the counsel of the Lord, building up the congregation in Word and doctrine.[8]

In addition, education is a requirement for the fully employed Seventh-day Adventist minister. Today, most, if not all, have undergraduate degrees. Many have graduate and post-graduate education and the Masters of Divinity degree is strongly encouraged. Educational training not only equips pastors for the task of ministry, but also enhances their interpersonal understanding of themselves and increases their capability for helpful resources in their own lives. Here is a brief history of the beginning of pastoral educational requirements.

In 1875, the first SDA College was established for the training of denominational workers, but not all the ministers came from that theological college. Some were called from various backgrounds. In later years candidates for the ministry were expected to have at least a college education with a degree in religion or its equivalent.

In 1929, the internship plan originated, which brought young ministers into the field after their preparatory theological course or its equivalent, for a period of two years' practical training under the leadership of experienced pastors and evangelists.

In 1953, by action of the General Conference, an additional year of academic training began to be required before the ministerial intern was ready for his fieldwork. In 1964, a further action was taken endorsing the Bachelor of Divinity degree as a requirement for SDA ministers. During a three-year internship the prospective minister would be supported from funds accruing from appropriations from the General, union, and local conferences; he would spend the first two years and two summers in the Seminary (of Andrews University) and the last year in intensive fieldwork.[9]

It must be understood by the Adventist minister in light of burnout and renewal that education is an essential process of learning about themselves and their profession.

It is important for the Adventist pastor to know and review their personal history so as to ascertain the foundation from which their ministry began, and to better focus on the future of their ministerial work. The Adventist minister, along with the assistance of the elders, plans for and leads out in all spiritual services of the church, such as the Sabbath morning church worship service, prayer meeting during the week, and leading out in the ordinances such as the communion service and baptism. Pastors ought to work in co-operation and in consultation with the duly elected officers of the church.[10] This is important to me because when there is a lack of communication and/or miscommunication with church leaders, misinformation is right behind, leading to more problems. Frustration mounts with the pastor when there is a task to be done and the assumption is that everyone has been informed regarding the task. In order to successfully delegate, open communication with the church leaders is essential for the pastor.

Because the pastor will be assigned to work in new cities and territories, there will rest upon them the responsibility of overseeing and fostering all branches of church work. Soul-winning endeavors through the Sabbath School, the Adventist Youth Society, the church school, the prayer meeting, as well as the Sabbath services, all come under the watchful care of the pastor. An ordained minister ranks above the local elders in leadership, and they should assist the pastor. The Adventist pastors' ordination qualifies them in the gospel ministry to function in all church rites and ceremonies; it is the pastors who should have charge of such services. They are to be the spiritual leader and adviser of the church. They are to instruct the church officers in their

> *The Adventist pastors' ordination qualifies them in the gospel ministry to function in all church rites and ceremonies.*

ministry assignments, give counsel and instruction in carrying out plans in all areas of church ministry and activity.[11]

BIBLICAL DEFINITION OF PASTORAL MINISTRY

Frustration and disillusionment in pastoral ministry can be the result of a non-descript job assignment with heavy responsibility. And because this job is so multifaceted, all encompassing, and complex by its very nature, it is imperative that the Adventist pastors understand the biblical role or "job description" of their office.

According to the Lexical Aids to the New Testament compiled and edited by Spiros Zodhiates, the word pastor comes from the Greek word "poimen" and is defined as "shepherd." This is "applied spiritually to Christ (Matt. 26:31; John 10:11,12,14,16; Heb. 13:20; 1 Peter 2:25) and also is given as designation for a spiritual pastor of the flock (Eph. 4:11.)"[12] But one still may ask, what does it mean to be a shepherd or pastor? For the sake of definition this is what a pastor should not be. Jesus said in *John 10:11-13* "I am the good shepherd: the good shepherd giveth his life for the sheep. But he that is an hireling, and not the shepherd, whose own the sheep are not, seeth the wolf coming, and leaveth the sheep, and fleeth: and the wolf catcheth them, and scattereth the sheep. The hireling fleeth, because he is an hireling, and careth not for the sheep." Good shepherds will give their life for their sheep, because each sheep has a place in the shepherd's heart. Hirelings do not have a love for the sheep, nor do they care about the sheep. It is just a job to the hireling. Hirelings only view their congregations as a means of climbing the corporate ladder; trying to get to the larger church, or they view the church only to fulfill their personal ambitions. Instead of loving, forgiving, and understanding the sheep, the hireling only controls and manipulates.[13]

> *Hirelings do not have a love for the sheep, nor do they care about the sheep. It is just a job to the hireling.*

The apostle Paul's writings in Ephesians chapter 4 lend great insight and clarity to this issue. His writings will also give pastors an understanding of their job description for their office of ministry. In delineating the spiritual gifts in Ephesians 4, the apostle Paul lists one of those gifts as that of a pastor. In fact, in Ephesians 4 Paul was primarily talking about the "people gifts" that the Lord had given to the church. These gifts included apostles, prophets, evangelists, pastors, and teachers. These gifts were given for a specific purpose, and were all basically clergy gifts.[14]

Paul assesses the role by stating "and he gave some, apostles; and some prophets; and some, evangelists; and some pastors and teachers; for the perfecting of the saints, for the work of the ministry, for the edifying of the body of Christ: Till we all come in the unity of the faith, and of the knowledge of the Son of God, unto a perfect man, unto the measure of the stature of the fullness of Christ" (Eph 4:11-13 KJV).[15]

Paul here indicates that the gifts have been given to the people for the church. These gifts are to endure until the church has reached the unity of the faith. This happens at the Second Coming of Jesus Christ.[16]

Many refer to Ephesians 4 to support the idea that the work of the ministry belongs solely to clergy. However, Russell Burrill, in his book Revolution in the Church, sheds light on the impact of the misplacement of the comma after "saints" in Ephesians 4 verse 12, as seen in the King James Version of the Bible. He states that the misplacement of the comma "creates serious consequences for our theology of the lay person and the pastor."[17] I agree wholeheartedly with Burrill's findings.

He states that "all modern versions of this text translate it far more accurately by eliminating the comma, which would make it read: "for the perfecting of the saints for the work of the ministry." In other words, the role of the pastor would be to perfect the saints for their ministry.[18] Burrill goes on to say that "this

> *This text is not describing the pastor as a performer of ministry, but instead as a trainer of ministers.*

text is not describing the pastor as a performer of ministry, but instead as a trainer of ministers." He then cites these textual translations as support of this description of the Biblical pastor.

Twentieth Century New Testament: To fit His people for the work of the ministry;

Weymouth's Translation: In order to fully equip His people for the work of service;

Williams Translation: For the immediate equipment of God's people for the work of service;

New English Bible: To equip God's people for work in His service;

Beck's Translation: In order to get His holy people ready to serve as workers;

Phillips Translation: His gifts were made that Christians might be properly equipped for their service.[19]

Burrill states that "all these translations make it abundantly clear that the biblical job description of the pastor is of one who trains and equips members for their ministry." Ministers in the New Testament are not just doers of ministry, but are also teachers and trainers of disciples. Training disciples to make other disciples is clearly seen as the role of the pastor in the New Testament.[20]

Therefore, the work of the pastor is biblically defined as essentially preparing and equipping God's people to do the work of the ministry. It is the job of the pastor to be a soul winner, but not the only soul winner in the church. It is the job of the pastor to do the work of the ministry, but not to be the only one that does ministry. Instead pastors are to train the members to do the work of the ministry. It is true that the pastor...performs ministry. They give vision, counsel, visit, encourage, teach, and organize, but whenever they do it alone, they act in the capacity of a layperson and are not functioning in the role as a pastor. In addition, to be in harmony with scripture the pastor should teach, train, and educate the members. If they do not function in this capacity, then biblically, they are not doing their job.[21] To be in harmony with the biblical definition of a pastor is to be in harmony with God. To be in harmony with God is the first and most essential step towards prevention of pastoral burnout or renewal from it.

VIEWS OF MISSION

Evangelism is foundational and essential to the life and work of the Adventist pastor. The need for the Adventist pastor to have a balanced view of church work and a clear understanding of mission is paramount to consistency and longevity in pastoral ministry. Pastors who view their mission or pastoral work unrealistically or inappropriately easily can become disillusioned and frustrated.

> *Evangelism is foundational and essential to the life and work of the Adventist pastor.*

First and paramount for Adventist pastors is the recognition and belief that their ministry is divinely appointed[22] and that it is God's purpose that the gospel message be preached to all the world. The Adventist pastor must understand that since Christ's ascension as the great Head of the church, they have been chosen ambassadors through whom He speaks and ministers to the needs of his children.[23] Divinely chosen, pastors must heed the mandate of the Saviour in *Mark 16:15*. He said to them, "Go into all the world and preach the good news to all creation." Therefore, the understanding of evangelism, whether personal or through a general world church perspective, is essential to maintaining a balance theologically and practically in pastoral ministry. If the pastors understanding of mission is unrealistic or their response to the great gospel commission is inappropriate, then an unhealthy imbalance of priorities will result. It is clear that the mission of the Seventh-day Adventist pastor is to spread the everlasting gospel of Jesus Christ, and his soon coming to the entire world. This mission is practiced through evangelism (meaning to teach others about Christ, discipling for Christ through Biblical doctrine or *teaching*), which results in baptisms of those who accept Jesus Christ as their personal Lord and Saviour and all that Adventists believe that Christ instructs us to follow.

Uniquely, in the Adventist pastorate, baptisms when viewed inappropriately or unrealistically become an end rather than the means of populating the kingdom of God. Pastors who view baptisms as a means for facilitating careers rather than building up the kingdom of God are at risk of becoming disillusioned with their work and at serious risk of becoming imbalanced. Many Adventist pastors feel pressured from within by their own internal calling to depopulate hell, and from without possibly by church members, or by conference leadership to maximize their baptisms. Baptisms are seen as a sign of a prosperous ministry, therefore the pressure—or as some would call it the incentive—to baptize many during a given year is paramount. If baptisms for the Adventist pastor become primary in their ministry, and teaching or indoctrination of individuals about Christ becomes secondary, then the pressure of success or failure increases. This all-consuming pronation towards baptisms as a career incentive, leads towards inevitable stress, frustration, and disillusionment caused by undue pressure. Even though the work should be done with all of our heart, mind, and soul, I have learned that the result is the Lord's and one must understand that in pastoral ministry the process of baptizing is one that will continue until Jesus returns. An erroneous view of baptism also distorts the pastor's measure of success in ministry because it views baptism as the end of the journey for the believer, rather than the beginning. Every pastor is not gifted as an evangelist. Some pastors are great teachers, administrators, missionaries, and some are great evangelists. Growth tends to be stifled when pastors work or continue to operate only out of their strengths or areas of giftedness. Baptisms are

> *An erroneous view of baptism also distorts the pastor's measure of success in ministry because it views baptism as the end of the journey for the believer, rather than the beginning.*

ongoing because millions still need to be reached for Christ, and not just by one pastor will they be reached, but by many pastors and laity.

HIRED OR CALLED

The issue of being called by God and hired by a conference can place a dilemma in Adventist pastors lives. Being called as pastors is a personal understanding as it relates to the mission and commitment to God's work in and on their lives. Being hired is seen in light of managing the small business we call the congregation. Thus it is very possible that the pastor, congregation, and the conference face this same dilemma; how to work and carry out its mandates. How should the Adventist pastors view themselves? How should the conference view the pastor? How should the congregation view their pastor?

When God calls a pastor to ministry, he first is calling them to spirituality and a personal relationship. This is a heavy responsibility and an awesome privilege. This call to spirituality is very personal in the walk with God. It must be established in private,

> *When God calls a pastor to ministry, he first is calling them to spirituality and a personal relationship.*

before it is manifested in a public way, because it is not anything that we initiated, but something that God initiated. This makes God the center of our lives.[24]

It is my opinion that the call of God in the life of the pastor is the personal acceptance of the inner yearning to be God's and to live for God. It is from the inner unction of the heart that a pastor's life long commitment to service springs forth. This calling gives reason and motivation for most pastors to serve. It is the relationship of the soul to God in service. Equipped with God-given gifts and a strong sense of willingness, the call demands a vertical reason and motivation to serve; that goes far beyond horizontal expectations. The reasons for serving as a pastor that only address earthy motivations will never be enough to keep pastors motivated. The Seventh-day Adventist Encyclopedia further elaborates on the work of the pastor by stating, "God has a church, and she has a divinely appointed ministry... Men appointed of God have been chosen to watch with jealous care, with vigilant perseverance, that the church may not be overthrown by the evil devices of

> *Equipped with God-given gifts and a strong sense of willingness, the call demands a vertical reason and motivation to serve; that goes far beyond horizontal expectations.*

Satan, but that she shall stand in the world to promote the glory of God among men."[25]

Since the call of God comes from God, and understanding that the pastor does not work in a vacuum, where should conviction be placed in the process of decision-making as an employee? Should all view the pastor as an employee of the conference, hired to do the work and carry out its mandates only, or does the pastor's personal conviction, vision, and direction matter?

"FINISHING THE WORK"

The "Great Gospel Commission" can be found in *Matthew 28:19-20*. This charges pastors to go, teach and baptize; a directive from our Lord and Savior Jesus Christ himself, and therefore evangelism or soul winning is what fulfills that directive. Uniquely, Adventists also proclaim the three angels messages of *Revelation 14:6-12* as a part of the everlasting gospel to be preached to an end-time world. The first angel proclaims to love God, and give Him glory for the judgment hour is come. The second angel's message proclaims that Babylon is fallen. The third angel's message proclaims that if anyone worships the beast and his image, or receives his mark, the same will be cast in the lake of fire. These messages, which are referred to as the everlasting gospel, are unique to Adventist preaching because they set forth an end-time proclamation of urgency. And not until the gospel has been preached to the world as a witness to all nations, will the end come according to *Mathew 24:14*. This has even prompted a coined phrase that is quite unique to the Adventist community. It is: "Finishing the work."

"Finishing the work" is captured in the Adventist pastor's end-time theology and remnant motif.

This is the phrase that Adventist pastors use in response to the great gospel commission. This actually means completing the work the Lord has called us to, so that we can finally make heaven our home and live with the Lord throughout the ceaseless ages of eternity. "Finishing the work" is captured in the Adventist pastor's end-time theology and remnant motif. Because of our prophetic belief that time is short, Adventist pastors have a sense of urgency to proclaim the gospel that many others do not. This work of evangelism or the preaching of the gospel to the end-time world causes some tension in the life of the Adventist pastor. Because as long as we are on earth and the Lord delays his coming, the work of the church continues. Therefore, the work of the pastor continues. Along with the sense of prophetic urgency, comes the feeling that there is always more ministry and more evangelism to be done. This causes for many in the Adventist ministry the tension of incompletion. It becomes paramount for the Adventist pastor to come to the realization that "finishing the work" through the preaching of the gospel, is truly God's work. "Finishing the work" is a term Adventist pastors use that may be perceived to indicate we have the sole responsibility to get the job done (evangelizing, baptizing, and spreading the gospel) so that the Lord will come. However, I differ from this philosophy. It is our job to do the work in its various facets, but the Lord has clearly stated in His word that He will finish it.

According to *Philippians 1:6* and *2:13*, it is God that starts a good work in you, and he will perform that work until Jesus returns again. We must be faithful to the work and the Lord will be faithful to perform and complete the work. Paul says in Philippians 1 verse 6, that being confident of this, that he who began a good work in you will carry it on to completion until the day of Christ Jesus. He also says in Philippians 2 verse 13, for it is God who works in you to will and to act according to His good purpose.

Pastors can never truly say that they have finished the work. In fact the only thing we can say that comes close, is to say what the apostle Paul said, "I have finished my course, I have kept the faith."[26] Correctly understanding their mission and duty will help Adventist pastors to pace themselves in ministry. Clearly understanding mission will cause the Adventist pastor to view baptisms differently. They will not be viewed solely as the facilitation of a career, but truly as a sacrament welcoming new believers and building up the kingdom of God. Clearly understanding mission will help the Adventist pastor to focus on the quality of their life and ministry.

Burnout's potential exists when mission is not viewed or perceived clearly. The words of a medical doctor while giving a young Adventist pastor a heart monitoring device, rang clearly when he declared, "Are you trying to bring on the Second Coming of Jesus Christ all by yourself?" In other words, the doctor was asking the pastor whether he was trying to finish the work all by himself.

> *Delegation will save the pastor from extinction.*

Delegation will save the pastor from extinction. The apostles definitely learned this the hard way. When they took on the load themselves of church work and spreading the gospel, the work was not accomplished. But then they delegated the portion of church work that they were not directly called to do. They gave themselves continuously to fasting and to prayer and to the ministry of the Word (Acts 6:4) and it resulted in a great increase of the spreading of the Word and to the increase of disciples.

Pastors who understand their role in fulfilling the great gospel commission will avoid frustration and being overwhelmed by the great task of ministry. The demand of the mission through time and care-giving require that the pastor be aware of spiritual vulnerability and physical signs of the burnout syndrome. Physical and chemical imbalances caused by overwork or undue stress will leave the minister physically, emotionally, and spiritually useless in the long run. Therefore delegation and planning is essential for the pastor in prevention of burnout.

CHAPTER

FLYING EMBERS
Prevention, Renewal, and Resources

4

He who labors as he prays
lifts his heart to God with his hands.

— Bernard of Clairvaux —

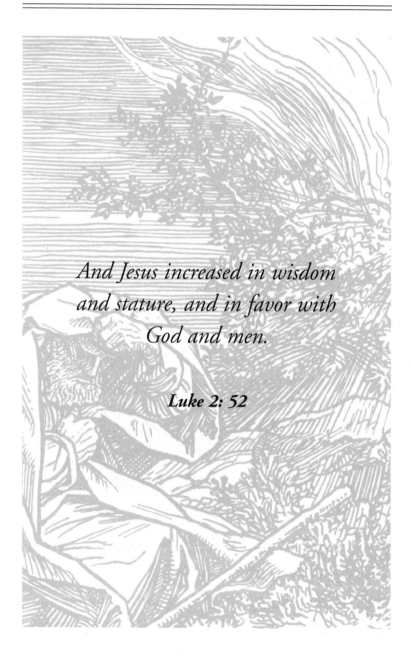

And Jesus increased in wisdom and stature, and in favor with God and men.

Luke 2: 52

FLYING EMBERS
Prevention, Renewal and Resources

*Cast all your anxiety on him
because he cares for you.*

1 Peter 5:7

Since pastors experience burnout in ministry, it is essential for Seventh-day Adventist pastors to use the resources available to them as a prescription for prevention and renewal. These specific resources are highly recommended as strategies through spiritual and practical steps.

It is understood in these contemporary days that the best form of care is preventive care. This is true for machinery, personal health, relationships, as well as pastors on

> *It is understood in these contemporary days that the best form of care is preventive care.*

their ministerial journey. Prevention is defined as anticipating by preparation or action beforehand.[1] Prevention for the pastor functions as a means of personal maintenance, feedback, and way to help monitor his or her wholeness (well-being spiritually, mentally, socially, and

133

physically). Without this personal care the pastor becomes vulnerable to the high-risk possibility of overload and frustration, which opens the door to burnout. Preventive maintenance is important to the wholeness of the Adventist pastor. Prevention is important because not all ministers' heed the danger signals, and not all of them have the same danger signals. As stated in chapter two, they may not even be aware of burnout's danger signals. For example, one pastor's loss of weight may signal that something is going on, while another's weight gain will signal the possibility of something, with neither pastor being aware of a problem. One pastor may withdraw from church members, while another may feel an increase in the need to be around church members in an attempt to hide the emptiness from his/her family. These varied responses are indicative of a lack of understanding and awareness of the effects of overload in ministry. Pastoral ministry practiced without personal preventive care can be extremely dangerous. Without prevention deliberately practiced, the pastor risks the possibility of eventually going through the motions of ministry without a real sense of passion and substance. In other words, functioning with a glass half full, or doing the job, but just getting by and not caring to improve can easily become the state of mind. Ultimately this may lead to the stunting of the congregation by allowing it to remain in mediocrity, unable to reach its full capacity for service through ministry.

Listen to the tone of the letter that one pastor wrote to another regarding his experience of going through the motions and eventually leaving the ministry.

We'll be leaving the pastoral ministry once and for all in a few days. My family, especially my wife, cannot continue to survive the continuous stress of a church. I must leave pastoral ministry to remain faithful to God, maybe to save my soul. I have felt so constrained by the politics of the whole thing that I have not been a spiritual leader. I am a titleholder. I do pastoral things. If I were to describe my church and denomination, I would say spiritually dead, yet physically functioning. Pulling the right strings without making waves has been a killer. I can say that if someone were not praying for us, I would walk away to call myself an atheist. In spite of people and problems, the Lord Jesus Christ has preserved my faith... Since speaking with my denomination leaders and fellow pastors, I find that five out of eight of us have been

*or are living under the same oppression. My
heart goes out to them. It amazes me that they,
too, do not go on to other ministries or secular
work. I have great compassion for them, for they
are in need.*[2]

After reading this letter, one may wonder whether this
pastor practiced burnout prevention or whether any
signs of exhaustion were recognized prior to his leaving.
Did this pastor even have resources that made it possible
to practice burnout prevention?

Admittedly, taking care of one's self has not been generally viewed as an essential priority for Christian living.
Indeed, giving any thought to one's self has been traditionally regarded with suspicion, even as inappropriate behavior for a faithful Christian disciple. Consequently, most of us learned that we should be quite careful about how we considered ourselves. The emphasis on self-care or maintenance was de-emphasized or misconstrued. I shall never forget hearing at the start of my ministry, over 18 years ago, a senior pastor bragging

> *Giving any thought to one's self has been traditionally regarded with suspicion, even as inappropriate behavior for a faithful Christian disciple.*

about the fact that he had not taken a vacation in years, implying that I should not take one anytime soon.

I agree with Brooks Faulkner's view on the prevention of burnout, or as he calls it "avoidance." He takes a three-dimensional view of one's personal image in ministry. This functional view for Faulkner is seen through mission, demands, and fulfillment. Mission for Faulkner is the pastor's first personal image of ministry, that portion of our over-all calling in which we most easily see ourselves succeeding. Mission must not be interpreted incorrectly, as though it were a call to take on all responsibility for the welfare of the entire congregation. This was discussed fully in chapter three. For Faulkner, individuals may not be clear—when the call into ministry is accepted—about what role or vocation of ministry God has in mind for them. There will be various roles to choose from in the process of becoming what God desires. Faulkner believes that these choices will be made as the minister's gifts become apparent. Once educational preparation is complete, the picture becomes clearer. Pastors will find themselves more comfortable doing some aspects of ministry than others. Even more complicating to the role of mission is that during ministry many pastors change roles during the pilgrimage. Staying focused on the mission is imperative to functional peace. This mission for Faulkner is also that which we would like to do with our role in ministry, and deciding when and where we will do the mission.[3]

The second part of the three-dimensional theory of burnout prevention in ministry vocation for Faulkner is to understand the demands on ministry. More specifically, pastors must be able to understand the demands, and be able to look at their own strengths and weaknesses with candor and realism. They must know what is demanded of them, and they must know whether they are capable of fulfilling these demands. Faulkner says that one of the most frustrating parts of his pastoral ministry was trying to meet the expectations of people who wanted a weekly pastoral visit. Some, he felt, needed to be visited each week and were honestly in need of pastoral care; these persons did not bother him. He would visit these persons gladly. However other parts of his ministry made demands on him that he met much less reluctance. He enjoyed the demands of sermonic preparation and hospital visitation. These were his favorite parts of the ministry even though they were demanding.[4] Faulkner discovered that by monitoring and understanding the various

> *Pastors must be able to understand the demands, and be able to look at their own strengths and weaknesses with candor and realism.*

demands, and understanding his own abilities to meet those demands helped him to use and preserve his energies wisely.

The third part of Faulkner's three-dimensional theory of avoiding burnout is fulfillment. He believes that the minister must find ways to be fulfilled as a person in order to continue to be effective in ministry. For Faulkner, to be fulfilled, means that pastors must know whether they are progressing or accomplishing goals. Progress, though difficult to measure in ministry, is still sought after in the work of the pastor. If the pastor does not see progress, it is difficult to feel a sense of fulfillment. Achievement is another way to measure fulfillment. If the pastor achieves his/her goals in ministry, Faulkner believes he/she can be fulfilled in ministry.[5] Therefore, burnout "avoidance" or burnout prevention is best realized or implemented when pastors understand their personal mission in ministry, when the demands on them are understood and regulated, and when a sense of fulfillment in ministry is achieved.

There are many resources available to help the Seventh-day Adventist pastors pace themselves and deliver some much-needed personal care for the prevention of pastoral burnout and the renewal from it. It is through spiritual renewal and the deliberateness of practical steps that pastors can be made whole. Many available resources exist in the local Seventh-day Adventist conferences. Even though these resources are varied, and implemented differently from conference to conference, they serve as excellent sources of strength for prevention and renewal.

> *It is through spiritual renewal and the deliberateness of practical steps that pastors can be made whole.*

STRATEGY FOR RENEWAL

Voices heard like, "I just want to be like one of the members. I'm tired of being on this pedestal that I didn't ask for." "You don't have to call me Elder or Pastor, just call me brother or sister_____, it's o.k." "I really don't care anymore. They aren't paying me enough to put up with all of this." "I'm not going back to that church…. they'll have to find someone else." "I don't have a sense of drive for evangelism anymore." "I really am just totally exhausted!" Though hypothetical, they are typical voices of pastors who have lost their desire to continue in the office of pastoral ministry. Their willingness to go on in ministry has faded. Their sense of vision and direction has been blurred. Their zeal has been squelched, and their efforts through administration, preaching, teaching, or evangelism when practiced, feel useless. They were once on fire! Ready to turn the world upside down. They had high expectations for themselves. They were dedicated, enthusiastic, and energetic. Where they enjoyed the presence of their church members, they now want to be alone and withdraw to themselves. Their passion for pastoral ministry is gone. Very often, they feel physically, spiritually, and emotionally drained. They may or may not recognize their feelings or their condition, but they are burned out. They need to be renewed.

Some clergy studies have shared that around 33 percent of clergy people have seriously considered leaving ministry because of its toll on them.[6] However, many have declared that they are too old and have too many years in the ministry to have to re-educate or receive training for another profession. Pastoral ministry, for many clergy people, is all they know. Other pastors have stated that deciding to leave felt as though they would be abandoning their call

> *Some clergy studies have shared that around 33 percent of clergy people have seriously considered leaving ministry because of its toll on them.*

from God, which in essence made them feel as if they would be leaving or turning their backs on the Lord, so they remained in pastoral ministry. They remained, even though they felt used up, as if they were simply going through the motions. They remained with no sense of real purpose or hope of ever being renewed again. But pastors can be renewed. They can, after burnout, be revived to start anew in pastoral ministry. Here are some spiritual steps and practical steps that can help the pastor move from burnout to renewal.

SPIRITUAL RENEWAL

It can be said that the pastor's work is never finished and that hard-working pastors need someone or something to help monitor their intensity. It is my recommendation that the Adventist pastor take a closer look at Jesus, because He is our greatest example of balance. *Luke 2:52* says, and Jesus grew in wisdom and stature, and in favor with God and men. (see Appendix 1) Jesus is our greatest and best example in holistic rest, and even more importantly He promises to give us rest.

> *Jesus is our greatest and best example in holistic rest, and even more importantly He promises to give us rest.*

142

For pastors, it is easy to conceal our alienation from God by our immersion in the busy things of God. While sincere activity like preaching, baptizing, visiting, praying with others, and presiding over church sacraments is good, it can coexist with an almost complete absence of private and personal presence with God.[7]

The best renewal that any pastor can have, ask, or think of is found in spiritual resources. Eugene H. Peterson, author of Under the Unpredictable Plant, insightfully described this connection when he said, "I do not find the emaciated, exhausted spirituality of institutional careerism adequate. I do not find the veneered, cosmetic spirituality of personal charisma adequate. I require something biblically spiritual rooted and cultivated in creation and covenant, leisurely in Christ, soaked in Spirit."[8]

When the apostles returned from their first missionary journey, the Saviour's command to them was,..."Come with me by yourselves to a quiet place and get some rest." *Mark 6:31.* They had been putting their whole souls into labor for the people, and this was exhausting their physical and mental strength. It was their duty to rest. Christ's words of compassion are spoken to His workers today just as surely as to His disciples. Come apart and rest awhile, He says to those who are worn and weary. It is not wise to always be under the strain of work and excitement, even in ministering to peoples spiritual needs; for in this way personal piety is neglected, and the powers of mind and soul and body are overtaxed. Self-denial is required of the servants of Christ, and sacrifices must be made; but God would have all to study the laws of health, and use reason when working for Him, that the life He has given may be preserved.

Though Jesus could work miracles, and had empowered His disciples to work miracles, He directed His worn servants to go apart into the country and rest. The Lord has given to every man his work, according to their ability, and He would not have only a few laden with responsibilities, while others have no burdens. The servants of Christ are not to treat their health indifferently. Let no one labor to the point of exhaustion, thereby disqualifying him or her for future effort. Do not try to crowd everything that is meant to be the work of two days into one. "In the end, pastors who work carefully and wisely will have accomplished just as much as those who expended their physical and mental strength so that they had nothing left to deposit, and nothing from which to draw in time of need.

> *Do not try to crowd everything that is meant to be the work of two days into one.*

The work of the Lord is worldwide, and He calls for every ounce of ability and power that we have. There is danger that His workers will abuse their powers as they see that the field is ripe for the harvest, but the Lord does not require this. After His servants have done their best, they may say, for he knows how we are formed, he remembers that we are dust. *Psalm103:14.*"[9]

Pastors who are called to give spiritual leadership to their community and to the broader world, are often found lacking the spiritual nurture needed for their service. The shift from the pastor providing the spiritual leadership to one of a managing director of the institution called church is probably one of the greatest challenges in the ministry. This role of pastor has been taken from a contemplative one characterized by prayer and meditation to one of varying degrees of more like the CEO or managing director.[10] Correspondingly, Andrew R. Irvine, author of <u>Living Between Two Worlds</u> says that "over 50 percent of pastors felt that to some degree people in the church wanted someone to run the show, not leaving time for personal spiritual nurture and some 65 percent indicated that to some degree they

> *65 percent indicated that to some degree they were often expected to give to others what they themselves lacked.*

145

were often expected to give to others what they themselves lacked."[11]

Therefore, it would seem appropriate for those who are called to the service of the Lord to begin reconstructing their identity with a redefined and healthy place for the spiritual to increase. Understanding this, the spiritual component of pastoral ministry must be given a place of identity with the minister. This calls for a shift in understanding that ministry is not solely a task—orientated profession but especially a spiritual role, which places the value equally on being as well as doing. The contemplative times are just as important in the life of the minister as are the active times of leadership such as in worship, pastoral visitation, and church administration. This shift of view sees the world giving just as much equal care to the practical—doing of ministry as it does to the spiritual—being world, and gives respect to that balance.[12]

> *The contemplative times are just as important in the life of the minister as are the active times of leadership.*

Irvine suggests that the development of the spiritual is difficult for the clergy. They are often so busy doing, that concern with being—the more devotional activity—seems impossible. Activism prevalent in the schedule of the clergyperson allows time only for prayer with others as part of the job and for scripture study in a search during the sermon process. For some pastors this necessary discipline of searching scripture may in and of itself provide some spiritual nurture, but it becomes a means to an end more often than not. Irvine argues that the attempt to create time for personal spiritual nurture simply adds more stress to the pastor, while the inability to maintain this discipline adds to the distress of feeling like a failure.

> *The attempt to create time for personal spiritual nurture simply adds more stress to the pastor, while the inability to maintain this discipline adds to the distress of feeling like a failure.*

Irvine is correct. Our need is not for more activity, even activity that is spiritual. Rather, the need is to shift the doing, to allow time and space for the spiritual. "The clamour of activism in the outer physical world, prompted by the clutter of unresolved issues in the inner world, prevents the development and nurture of the spiritual which must transcend both worlds. There is a need to remove the clutter so that in the midst of all of life the transcendent spirit can be experienced."[13] Busyness in ministry is often the veneer cover used to place over the already existing cluttered life of the pastor.[14] Church work—attending meetings, setting up tables, and setting up office computers often crowds out the real work of the church—the saving of souls for the kingdom.

Spiritual renewal therefore, is not focused on the doing of spirituality, but rather the daily practice of being in close relationship to God. It is realizing and knowing who God is and who you are in that relationship. To be spiritually renewed means to depend less on the horizontal relationships and more on the vertical. To be spiritually renewed is to start over again, to be drawn closer to the Lord, to be revived supernaturally. Jesus gave the great invitation to each pastor in Matthew 11:28-30 when He said, "Come to me, all you who are weary and burdened, and I will give you rest. Take my yoke upon you and learn from me, for I am gentle and humble in heart, and you will find rest for your souls. For my yoke is easy and my burden is light."

PROFESSIONAL SPIRITUALITY AND PERSONAL SPIRITUALITY

It may be helpful to distinguish here between professional spirituality and personal spirituality. It is apparently quite possible for many clergy to live their spiritual lives almost exclusively in the public or communal mode of liturgical prayer, preaching, teaching, and ministering to others. This spirituality might be called professional in the sense of being the official, ecclesial expression of Christian faith. In itself, it is precious and so is the clergy person's expression of it. Evoking it from others is a major part of his/her special ministry to the life of the Body. On the other hand, a clergy person who almost completely neglects times of silence, meditation, and personal prayer is very likely to leave his/her own personal relationship to God in the obscure background of awareness. Donald Hands and Wayne Fehr, in their book <u>Spiritual Wholeness for Clergy: A New Psychology of Intimacy with God, Self, and Others</u>, describe this perilous possibility of pastors losing their grip of spirituality in their relationship with God by saying:

> *Clergy who pray only on the run, in preparation for preaching and other ministries, or with others (in a clerical role) are unlikely to recognize or express their own actual feelings toward God. They tend to relate to God only in the role of worship leader and teacher and counselor for others. They do not let their private pain or personal struggles be part of their relationship with*

God. Also, they hardly ever allow God's unique and personal leading of their own lives to be perceived. They are not listening to God very much.[15]

The quest for true intimacy with God by the clergy person is a matter of spirituality that is personal. Spirituality means a concrete way of living in conscious relationship to the mystery of God. That which is specific and unique to an individual is personal. Each person's story is different, yet related to the great story told by the church, generation after generation.

> *Spirituality means a concrete way of living in conscious relationship to the mystery of God.*

The ordained pastor ought be aware of his or her own personal story in order that it may be honored. Talking about the personal spirituality of the professional minister, moreover, places the emphasis on that person's humanity and needs. This is often neglected or even repressed under the pressures of helping others. The crucial point for the clergy person is to consider whether they have a personal life or unique relationship with God, otherwise they will be defined by the ministry that is carried out to others. The tendency for many clergy is to practice the second option. Those who allow ministry given to others to define them will neglect themselves and operate in a compulsive manner. Anyone who gives priority to a personal spirituality this way will gradually come to discover and appreciate the great value it has for a fulfilled life and an effective ministry.[16]

PRAYER LIFE

Anyone serious about living a spiritual life will devote time to personal prayer, time to relate to God in one's own name, not as official worship leader or minister to others. What seems to be crucial for spiritual deepening and growth is a discipline of silence. One needs to become outwardly and inwardly quiet, without an agenda, in reverent openness to the blessed Mystery. The most basic attitude of prayer involves settling quietly into one's own center of quiet discipline in silent presence to God. Keeping themselves so busy with their ministry to others that they hardly ever settle into quiet presence to themselves and to God is often an avoidance of self-knowledge because of some disorder they

> *The most basic attitude of prayer involves settling quietly into one's own center of quiet discipline in silent presence to God.*

are reluctant to consider.[17] "For clergy, the daily practice of contemplative prayer is bound up with a healthy and much-needed attitude of legitimate self-care. This is the attitude of Sabbath, the reverent and joyful celebration of our very life as given to us by God."[18] So that renewal may be a lasting rich experience, the practice and teaching of prayer in their congregations will ensure the richness of their spirits and prayers. Renewal from pastoral burnout really begins and ends with the pastor's spiritual life.

PRACTICAL STEPS

It is through the school of practical learning that the Adventist pastor can find renewal again from burnout. Simple steps like eating sensibly. Getting a good breakfast and avoiding greasy foods and fast foods filled with bad cholesterol, eating low calorie meals that are high in energy, and even supplementing your meal with vitamins and minerals will go a long way. Learning to make deliberate attempts to relax, by getting away from the phone, sitting in a comfortable chair with closed eyes, and making deliberate efforts to relax all your muscles is another practical step towards renewal. Other steps may include planning a sensible exercise program, sticking to a regular sleep schedule, and disciplining ones self to withdraw. One of the most disturbing phone calls ministers receive are those that acknowledges that it is their day off, but the caller still needs to speak or meet with them. Another step toward renewal is to establish a feedback system.[19]

Even though Adventists emphasize healthful living and Adventist pastors preach about the virtues of living a temperate lifestyle, eating and laboring intemperately is prevalent.

> *Even though Adventists emphasize healthful living and Adventist pastors preach about the virtues of living a temperate lifestyle, eating and laboring intemperately is prevalent.*

Those who make great exertions to accomplish just so much in a given time, and continue to labor when their judgment tells them they ought to rest, are never gainers. They are expending a force that they will need at a future time. When the energy that they have so recklessly used is called for, they fail, because it was previously used. Physical strength is gone, and mental power is unavailable; their time of need has come, and their resources are exhausted. Each day brings its responsibilities and duties, but the work of tomorrow must not be crowded into the hours of today. God is merciful, full of compassion, reasonable in His requirements. He does not ask us to pursue a course of action that will result in the loss of physical health or the enfeebling of the mental powers. He would not have us work under pressure and strain to the point of exhaustion.

There is need that God's chosen workers should listen to the command to go apart and rest awhile. Many valuable lives have been sacrificed because of disregard of this command. There are those who might be with us today, to help forward the work both at home and in the mission fields, if they had but realized before it was too late. The field is large and the need for workers great, yet they felt that at any cost they must press on. When nature uttered a protest, they paid no heed, but doubled the work they should have done.

Laborers under the heavy pressure of pastoral care and anxiety, and are overworked in both body and mind, would be better to turn aside and rest awhile, not for selfish gratification, but that they may be better prepared for future duties. The enemy of our souls is ever on our track, ready to take advantage of our every weakness that would help to make his temptations effective. When the mind is overstrained and the soul is wearied with toil, when the body

> *To turn aside and commune with Jesus is the shield of rest to every believer.*

is enfeebled, Satan presses upon the soul with his fiercest temptations. To turn aside and commune with Jesus is the shield of rest to every believer. Those who do not labor however, have no need of rest.

It was to those worn down in His service, not to those who were always sparing themselves, that Christ addressed His gracious words. And today it is to the self-forgetful, those who work to the very extent of their ability, who are distressed because they cannot do more, and who in their zeal go beyond their strength, that the Saviour says, come away and rest a while. Let this be a lesson for all in the army of faith under the training of the Lord. God is desirous to reveal in the pastor's life a life that is in conflict with the world, its customs or its practices, and every one needs to have a personal experience in obtaining knowledge of the will of God. Be still, and know that I am God. (Psalm 46: 10). Ellen White speaks of this quiet as the only place to find true rest and the most effective environment in which we prepare to do God's work. "Amid the hurrying throng, and the strain of life's intense activities, the soul that is thus refreshed will be surrounded with an atmosphere of light and peace. The life will breathe out fragrance, and will reveal a divine power that will reach men's hearts."[20]

Other practical steps to help pastors renew will include working toward integration of activities to reflect their real values. Many clergy are suffering from a lack of integration in their lives. What is typically seen in ministry is the split – off, public self or the façade or glittering image that is maintained with great effort, and not much thought. This lifestyle is one of control in ministry and, in one sense, control of image management. Such people are split between head and heart, public and private, professional and personal life.[21] Another practical step may include the need to practice introspection; meaning to look at one's self, by looking at the past. Knowing one's family history personally is to be aware of the issues, tendencies, limita-

> *Knowing one's family history personally is to be aware of the issues, tendencies, limitations, and legacies one must face in any rebirth experience.*

tions, and legacies one must face in any rebirth experience.[22] To know yourself is to be set free.

A person's energy must also have a source, just as a lake must have a source. A human being cannot always pour energy out; there must be times when energy comes back in. Ebb tide must be followed by high tide, nutrients taken from the soil as we grow our food must be replaced, and the energy that goes out of us must also be replenished. Life provides us with many sources of energy; however, it is fitting to mention some of the places where we can look for new sources of energy, as described in six steps by John Sanford. He suggests that a change in the pastor's outer activity, meaning to begin practicing different activities from those of the pastor's regular line of work will enhance capabilities to regain energy. Having relationships that are based on personal friendship, instead of the recurring professional level is another method of regaining and renewing energy. Understanding that the body and spirit are closely related, Sanford reminds pastors to use the body creatively to bring about physical rejuvenation, so that as the body is revived, so to is the spirit. He also suggests spiritual meditation, logging or recording one's hopes or dreams, and keeping a ministry journal as other forms of regaining energy in ministry.[23]

Ultimately regaining energy, or being renewed, is dependent upon the minister's reliance upon God. Dependence on the Lord to manage the pastoral life and the lives of others is essential to restoration. Pastors who are presently under a great deal of stress, even fearing the possibility of burnout, are also near to an important truth for themselves: they need the Lord fully in their lives. Indeed, nothing less than an act of surrender can release one from the burden of feeling indispensable and the drive to be in charge. Only spiritual surrender permits the letting go of anxieties that have all the appearances of urgent emergencies. But that surrender is possible because the good news is that Christ is Lord, and pastors do not need to hold onto the burden of trying to run everything.

Many people today affirm their spiritual surrender by praying the Serenity Prayer: "God grant me the serenity to accept the things I cannot change, courage to change the things I can, and wisdom to know the difference." Paul adequately addressed our modern plight from an ancient prison cell in Rome. His body bore many scars and he was under the threat of losing his life, when he wrote:

> *I have learned, in whatever state I am, to be content. I know how to be abased, and I know how to abound; in any and all circumstances I have learned the secret of facing plenty and hunger, abundance and want. I can do all things in him who strengthens me. (Phil 4: 11b-13)*

Paul was kindly trying to reassure his friends that, despite the severity of his circumstances, he had more than enough resources for meeting the stress in his life.[24]

If pastors could make such a statement so confidently, their lives would be healthy, balanced, rewarding, holy, and producing wonderful results in ministry. If pastors could speak these words with joy and assurance, this book would not have needed to be written.

THE SABBATICAL

The Sabbatical is a resource available in the practice of preventive care and renewal for the Seventh-day Adventist pastor. Why a Sabbatical? Because church members often see the exciting part of being a pastor such as chairing the church board or business meetings, preaching, marrying couples, as well as related activities, but the fact is that being a pastor involves many hours every week of very high pressure although routine work, running from one hospital to another, trying to prepare sermons, etc. One problem church members often forget is that usually the Sabbath is one of the busiest days for the pastor. Preaching, visitation, and attending potlucks are all a part of Sabbath ministering; still they take away from alone time and family time. In

> *One problem church members often forget is that usually the Sabbath is one of the busiest days for the pastor.*

some ways this is paradoxical to Adventist Sabbatarian theology. Sabbath worship, from sundown Friday to sundown Saturday commemorates for Seventh-day Adventists the worship of the true God as Creator of heaven and earth, the sea and all that in them is *Exodus 20:11.* Honoring the Sabbath, means to worship the Lord of the Sabbath who rested, blessed, and sanctified the seventh day as a perpetual memorial of His great creation *Revelation 14:7b.* The paradox is that for the Adventist pastor the day of spiritual rest and worship is when most of his/her personal resources are given out through service and ministry. While it is lawful to do good on the Sabbath, and while it was our Lord's custom to be in the synagogue on the Sabbath day, the Adventist pastor must be on guard to find personal fulfillment and joyful balance in not only being a blessing to others on Sabbath, but to be blessed personally on Sabbath. In other words, while saving others, pastors must make sure that they are not cast away.

In order that renewal and regeneration are available to the Adventist pastor, sabbatical time would be beneficial. This by the way, not only benefits the pastor, but also greatly benefits the congregation! Several congregations whose pastors have taken sabbaticals have been amazed at the changes in preaching, prayer meetings, and other church programming when their pastors returned, rejuvenated and full of new and fresh idea. All of us need time to be alone, alone with our families, and alone with God. Since pastors are the spiritual head of the congregation, it is especially important for them to have this time.[25]

The sabbatical is not meant to be vacation! The sabbatical should not generally be connected with vacation time nor is it intended to be a time of study or for the sole purpose of intellectual pursuits. Rather, its objective is to take time for renewal and spiritual regeneration. A sabbatical should involve five specific areas that include first, a time for personal and family renewal. This is for the purpose of reconnecting and reestablishing true one on one relationships that go much deeper than just surface living or involvement in the same house. Secondly, the sabbatical should include physical, intellectual, and emotional restoration that will help to improve the pastor's functionality, spirituality, and personal introspection. The sabbatical should include time for the pastor to develop in new areas professionally. Professional growth is essential in the process

> *The sabbatical should not generally be connected with vacation time nor is it intended to be a time of study or for the sole purpose of intellectual pursuits.*

of renewal because it allows the pastor to be stretched by others, and it takes the pastor out of the repetitive cycles of the week. It should be a time for spiritual growth in order that the pastor may experience brand new personal revelations with God. Spending time away and alone with God is like recharging car batteries when they have run down. One needs to walk with God in order to walk with His people. Also, sabbaticals should be taken to interact with peers, colleagues, and those in the same professional journey. So often pastors find themselves far more isolated than the congregation understands. Pastors need time to visit with other pastors, to attend other churches, to get some unique perspectives that will help them break out of the pastoring year by year cycle.[26]

While procedures will vary from one church to another, a general format of the sabbatical implementation would be helpful. Meeting with the church leaders about your sabbatical is essential to the support needed in taking this step. A pastor desiring a sabbatical should put together a short proposal and share this with his/her head elder. If the head elder is supportive, then it should be presented to the board of elders at a more formal meeting for their support. Once this is done, if the leaders agree with the proposal, or the proposal is modified by some of the church leaders' input, then the next step is to present it to the church board. At this point it is essential that, prior to the church board presentation, a plan be in place to cover all duties, services, and emergencies. A good idea is to have these duties covered by the associate minister, retired pastor, practicing pastors of nearby congregations, or by local church elders. It is suggested that the pastor's proposal to the board include dates, the individuals who will be speaking, and their phone numbers, so the head elder or anyone needing to contact the individuals from the church can contact them. In the case of an associate pastor, this of course does not apply. It will be important to the church board to know that the pastor is concerned and understands that the church will still continue to function, and function as efficiently as possible. A follow-up plan is important in ministry areas such as Bible studies, family involvement, counseling, visitation, etc. It is crucial that these individuals be contacted, and even introduced to the individuals that will continue on during the pastor's sabbatical.

At the church board meeting the head elder should present the proposal to the board to see if they are interested in supporting the proposal. If they are, then the videotape should be shown. If they are in concurrence with moving on with the proposal, then the next procedure should be handing out manuals to the church board to study during the next month.

Next the pastor may want to set up a small committee chaired by the head elder to organize and sharpen up the proposal to be brought to the church board next time. If there is adequate support at this time, the process of filling out the sabbatical forms should take place. After this, have another church board meeting to study the proposal; and the forms that have been proposed by the small committee meeting with the pastor should be reviewed as well. Once approved, the proposal should be sent to the Ministerial Director of the Conference for the final approval, at least two months in advance.[27]

The length of the sabbatical will vary from conference to conference, but a three-month sabbatical is not abnormal. Some conferences allow up to four weeks for every two years of pastoral work and some allow this time to accrue up to one quarter of a year or three months, at the rate of two weeks per year, after the first two years. In most cases a shorter sabbatical is encouraged and appropriate.

VACATIONING

A vacation is an essential resource for the pastor and the family in the practice of preventive care. Every conference has a policy for vacation for its employees. Vacations are just as essential for the family of the pastor as it is for the pastor.

The demands on pastors call for a vacation away from it all. Vacations taken at home are usually not real vacations. Getting away, coming aside from the vicinity is as important as declaring that you are taking a vacation. Imagine if Jesus were pastoring today, He "would have had five reporters with him when he went into the garden to pray. He would have had a group of television reporters and newsmen following Him into the upper room. If He lived today, He could not have withdrawn to regain His strength."[28] The pressures from without, such as deadlines, meetings, and family crises do not make it easy for the modern pastor to get away. One minister's story solidifies this point:

> I went on vacation last year to Myrtle Beach. We had a condominium rented for nine days. On the second day, I received a call. One of the deacons who was prominent in our church had died. Naturally, I went back for the funeral. While I was there (I had left my wife in Myrtle Beach), the widow asked me to help with the soliciting of a lawyer. The estate was sticky and the church was involved. Finally, I sent for my wife. No rest for the devoted.[29]

Vacationing is not only a form of family care, health, and wholeness, but vacationing is a form of burnout prevention.

Vacationing is not only a form of family care, health, and wholeness, but vacationing is a form of burnout prevention. My grandfather, who is a retired Adventist pastor shared with me early on in my ministry that he would go away once a quarter from the church, and only the head elder would know where he and his family had gone. Vacations are to be cherished and taken. Even though some vacation policies allow for days to be carried over year to year, the importance of getting away to refresh and renew one's self is paramount to well being; therefore, allowing vacations to accrue is not conducive to good health.

SUPPORT NETWORKS

A thriving ministry does not occur by osmosis, but it does occur through support. I have found peer feedback to be extremely important for personal growth and in the prevention of exhaustion. Learning from the experience of others helps ministers to learn more about themselves. Support networks such as ministerial fellowships, counselors, mentors, educators, intimate friends, professional support, helping acquaintances, challengers etc. are all ways of support that should be accessed. For prevention, pastors should listen to their families; they are exceptional mirrors of the needs of pastors. Pastors should also be willing to receive feedback from their congregation, which has the tendency to be real honest. "Though they may not show it, pastors need lay leaders to be aware of the causes of burnout, to watch for signs of it, to give them permission to avoid burnout, and to initiate the recovery process when the problem begins to show."[30]

In spite of the underlying barriers to gaining support, most clergy and their spouses do have some support. Barbara Gilbert, found out some general observations about pastoral support systems through questionnaires and surveys. She found that there is not just any one way of getting support. Different methods work differently for individuals, based on the nature of the issue. She also found that external circumstances determine where people will be influenced to find support such as, having a spouse or not, or living in an urban versus a rural area. Pastors truly determined to attain and maintain personal and professional health will find healing relationships "because they value supportive relationships enough to give them some priority." Many pastors are open to such support "only after breaking free from some of the personally limiting issues." Ordinary social and professional activities bring together people who are able to form a mutually supportive relationship. But even in these situations, some "initiative and some intentionality" is required that will foster the relationship. Such relationships are usually not hastily formed. "Trusted relationships take time and commitment."[31]

It is important to stress that the development of support is not a single act nor can it occur only at one level if it is to be effective. A single source of support, because of our diverse needs and demands, may fail to live up to our expectations. An example is the ministerial professional group which, when expected to be the primary support for clergy at all levels, fails at the levels of personal and pastoral support. We have recognized in the preceding chapters that imbalance among vocational priorities, unrealistic expectations, relational conflicts, and superficial views of mission exist in different forms and at different levels. Each is important and each requires different dynamics of support in order to satisfy the need for support. To view these specific needs in a general way is so imprecise that it is of no value. Equally, to seek support that is too narrow and precise will not satisfy the diversity of support.

Support, therefore, must develop and be available on multiple levels. This places the responsibility on all entities involved; from those at the professional, denominational, local community and church level to the individual minister; to assure that such support structures are available. The onus, however, is ultimately on the individual to utilize the support available.[32] It is through the use of these resources that the Adventist pastor can thrive while on the battlefield for the Lord. (see Appendix 2)

TO BE MADE WHOLE

Following the biblical model of wholeness as seen through the life of God's Son, Jesus Christ, is imperative. The biblical model of wholeness is expressly seen through Jesus as a ministering instrument. Jesus is one with the Father and He desires not to live out His will, but desires to live out the will of His Father. Jesus was the express wholeness of God made flesh. The Bible says in Luke 2:52, that Jesus grew in wisdom (he grew—mentally), and stature (He grew—physically). He was in favor with God (He was in right relationship with the Father—spiritually). He was in favor with man (He was in right relationship with humanity—socially). Jesus is the perfect example for each pastor to follow and if we neglect any part or area of our Lord's example of wholeness, we risk becoming unbalanced and thereby sabotaging our ability to reach God's ideal for us.

Wholeness, in the biblical sense, is different from the medical model of health, the capitalistic model of accumulation and comfort, the success model of achievement and status, or the psychiatric model of freedom from psychosis and neurosis. Biblical wholeness is a very special understanding of a human being. True wholeness does not occur until one learns how to live out the real meaning of "not my will, but thine be done". Biblical wholeness is not an end in itself. Its function and value lie in using wholeness for the corporate good. We are whole when we are forgiven, loved, and serving God, not just when we feel good and are without problems.

> *True wholeness does not occur until one learns how to live out the real meaning of "not my will, but thine be done".*

Wholeness, in the biblical sense, not only includes suffering and pain but also suggests that we learn and grow through failures and hurts. This not only legitimizes these experiences; it also denies the contemporary American dream of full health, wealth, and happiness as the goal of living. This concept of wholeness does not make pain attractive but it helps us accept, understand, and grow through our pain.

The body, mind, and spirit dimensions of self—awareness and self—nurture do not imply a fragmentary self, but these categories may focus our self—care more specifically. Each category is interdependent. For example, we cannot ignore the physical care of the body and not experience some deficit in the health of the spirit. We need to learn that caring for the body means meeting its basic needs, not indulging in all of its learned wants. Bodily nurture involves commonsense, nutrition, exercise, change of pace, work, and rest.

The second leg of the support stool is our intimate relationships with God and humanity. As pastors, we often feel like we already spend enough time with people. Sometimes we feel that there is not enough time for work, much less just sitting and socializing with family or friends. Such feelings are misleading. We need the kind of relationships in which we are just persons with the same needs and joys as others. Time spent in such relationships is not wasted or optional. This is valuable time in keeping us human and in preventing us from developing a distorted view of others and ourselves. Such time is certainly valuable to those with whom we have intimacy commitments (*1 Timothy 3*). The nurture of the spirit completes the wholeness trilogy: body, mind, and spirit. It is the third leg of our support stool.

Pastors sometimes neglect nurturing the spirit and developing a spiritual discipline that establishes a relationship with God. We may feel that we have had so much theology in seminary that we do not need to study it seriously anymore. We may feel that Scripture reading and individual prayer are things to be done only in sermon preparation and for the professional functions, because we feel that the real work of ministry is out there working with people,[33] but this is not the case at all. We cannot give what we do not have. Intimacy with Christ can be faked, but for so long. The secret to any authentic viable ministry is to know the living Lord personally and intimately. "Never in human history were pastors more needed than now. In a time when personal and public sins have strangled satisfaction out of life, there is a crying need for someone like a pastor to put broken people in touch with the Author of authentic wholeness."[34]

In conclusion, renewal means to be restored back to the original state. The burned out pastor through prayer and communion can achieve renewal with God. Through the daily practices of the methods spelled out in this book, the burned out pastor and the at-risk pastor, can now pray Frances Ridley Havergal's prayer:

> *"Let me then be always growing,*
> *Never, never standing still;*
> *Listening, learning, better knowing*
> *Thee and Thy most blessed will."*[35]

APPENDIX 1

JESUS
Luke 2:52 Axioms of Balance

Wisdom (Mind)	Stature (Body)
• Yearning for the deep things of God • Meditation upon God's Word • Not double-minded	• Physical Well-Being • In Health
God (Spiritual)	**Man (Social)**
• Essential and Vital Connection for Victorious Living • Creator and Source of all Abundant Life	• Genuine concern for others based on God's value • Willingness to get involved to help the human plight

APPENDIX 2

Ministry Care Line
800-767-8837
— CONFIDENTIAL CONVERSATIONS —
Service of Kettering Clergy Care
Mon.–Fri. 2:00-5:00 p.m.*   Mon.–Thurs. 8:00-11:00 p.m.*
*Eastern Standard Time

For more clergy resources contact
Brighter Hope Ministries, Inc. at **www.brighterhope.org**.

PASTORAL INTERVIEW

I conducted an interview with an Adventist pastor who had experienced the pastoral burnout syndrome. This pastor led a congregation that grew from 100 to 500 members and built a multi-million dollar church plant, all in less than 10 years. Because of its toll on his health, the strain of having to work two jobs (for his son's health reasons), and because of the continuous non-stop repetitive nature of pastoral work, this pastor chose to leave pastoral ministry for approximately one and a half years. However, he is back in pastoral ministry today and is pastoring with a greater awareness of the signs and symptoms of burnout. He is renewed! Praise the Lord!

Question: *What does the term "finishing the work" mean to you? It is a term we use often as Adventist pastors, but what does this mean to you personally?*

Pastor: *I perceive "finishing the work" as becoming complete or mature in Christ. It's growing up into the full stature of Christ. I do not see it so much as an outward work. I know that a lot of people do see it as going around the world, covering the entire globe, I know it will be that. But I see it more as an internal experience that all true believers will experience. They will grow up fully in the stature of Christ, having the love of Christ, the patience of Christ. As this takes* *place, then the true church will come to reflect Jesus Christ, and when the true church on earth reflects Jesus Christ, then he will come for His own.*

Question: *So you see God finishing the work instead of ministers finishing the work?*

Pastor: *Exactly, as it is stated in Scripture, greater is He that is in us, than he that is in the world. Well He that is within us, is doing something through us. What He is doing is cleansing, as you know, purifying, and getting us ready to live among all the other holy beings in heaven.*

Question: *How many years have you been in the pastoral ministry in the Adventist church?*

Pastor: *I've been in pastoral ministry for seventeen years.*

Question: *Can you tell me a little bit about your personal journey beginning in ministry? Briefly, tell me when you began, some of your dreams, goals, and aspirations.*

Pastor: *Well, initially coming out of school with a BA in Theology, I was asked to serve as a Youth Pastor with Pastor _____; and I was with him for only about four months and after that there wasn't a position for me.*

This was somewhat a wilderness experience. During that wilderness experience, which was about a year long, I never doubted God's call in my life, but I just wondered what was He doing. I guess it was the same with Moses, when he went 40 years without a pastor.

Then the following year I became a Bible teacher, which I also consider ministry, it seems if you are teaching Bible or preaching Bible you're still ministering; and the year after that I became an Associate Pastor for three years and after that I became a Senior Pastor. Some of my dreams have always been to really personally get as close as I could to God. Believing that we all influence each other, I felt that if my connection with him was strong enough, I could help improve other people's connections. I think it vain of me to ask people, or to encourage people to have a close walk with God if I don't have that close walk myself. I believe that anyone who has a close walk with God will shine his light before men. People will see their good works and glorify God by those good works.

I'm not thinking, once again outwardly, the outward manifestation of say building a church, baptizing a 1000 people but, when I think of letting your light shine, I think of the light of Jesus Christ [that] will shine within us and those are some of my main dreams and visions.

To have the gentleness that Jesus has while at the same time have the strength and conviction to do what His Father says to do and with humility, patience and confidence; those are my real personal dreams.

Question: **You know I am studying the subject of Pastoral Burnout in the Adventist Church, and I know that you did leave pastoral ministry for a period of time and I want to talk to you about that for a few minutes.**

Could you share some of your reasons, or experiences that lead you to deciding to leave pastoral ministry? What were some of the causes, did you feel like you were stressed, dealing with issues?

Pastor: *I am still reflecting on that journey, but I would like to say this, as a back drop, for approximately seven years, I taught school full time and I pastored full time and while pastoring and teaching full time we were* *also building a new $2 million dollar church and so at the same time when I was doing this, I took a college course to get my administrative credentials to be a principal. I don't know.* (Note: This pastor taught school full time so that his child could have full health coverage for a chronic disease.)

Response to Pastor: *You were doing a lot.*

Pastor: *Yes! Yes, and in doing those things, sometimes you've not even conscious of the stress that you're under. When you really feel mission oriented you kind of do whatever needs to be done. Of course there was a strain on my family, which was not that obvious or noticeable. My wife, whom the Lord has blessed to have her own life, is now a school teacher, but a lot of times she is away from home, between these various jobs and things.*

But to make a long story short, something happened to me in which my focus changed, my original focus was very simple when I became pastor of the church, we had 90 members on the books and about 25 attending. So the initial mission was, okay let's build up the church and we did not have a church building. So the thing was souls and a place to stay, it was that simple and the Lord blessed and we went from 90 members to over 500 members in a matter of approximately 7 years. And during that time we were renting other facilities and then we finally rented a gymnasium. Our goals were let's build the body of Christ numerically speaking, and build up the body of Christ as far as a facility to worship in was concerned.

And once those two major goals were reached, where we had built up the body physically and we had the number of people and we had this church and as it were the outer trappings of successful ministry, while at the same time I must confess that I was not running the church, I could never do it. Of course it's the Lord that does, but I was not even running my life, it seemed that I was being run. It was one meeting to the next, one project to the next, one seminar to the next, one sermon to the next. I realized that this is not how I wanted to spend the rest of my life. So I started to do some internal inventory and I realized that I needed to get back to a real relationship with God. Not that I didn't feel I had a real relationship, but the relationship was not the quality that I wanted it to be. And it came to the point where I didn't know exactly what to do, but I knew what not to do and what not to do was, to not continue doing what I was doing.

So it just happened that at the same time when I was coming to this dilemma, that our conference was actually asking people if they wanted to be laid off. They were going to lay 10 people off and they didn't know who they wanted to lay off, but they knew there were people who wanted to stay in the ministry, who they considered laying off.

And between what the conference was doing and what I was feeling, I thought this was an ideal time for me. I'll volunteer to be one of those to be let go. And so when I approached the conference with this, they didn't try to talk me out of it, and when they didn't try to talk me out of it, I said well I guess everybody will be happy. If I just step out of that [out of pastoral ministry]. So that's what took me to that point of actually stepping away from that [pastoral ministry] and what happened of course, as soon as I did that, the Lord took me back to where I began with him which was teaching Bible in a private school once again. The ministry really didn't stop; it more or less changed; so I went from pastoring to teaching Bible.

Question: *Would you say that the level of stress or the load lightened when you just taught, instead of pastoring?*

Pastor: *Oh tremendously, and I might say physiologically speaking I didn't even realize what was happening. I went on a missionary journey to the island of Madagascar in 1997, I didn't even realize the stress I was under. 1997 was the year I actually stepped out of pastoring fulltime and that same summer I went to Africa as a missionary and came back and I got sick, and I didn't realize the level of the sickness.*

The fall of that year I came down with pneumonia, and I'm a person who rarely gets sick, and so I knew that pneumonia was a very serious illness, but I did not even realize what my body was going through, so that sickness was a sign to me that I was really overdoing it. Something was really off.

Question: *So, you did recognize then, that there was some strain physically on you?*

Pastor: *Oh yes, yes. When I first started pastoring, the I had no gray hair either. Warning pastor, warning!* (Laughter)

Question: *In the Adventist church there is a unique relationship between what the conference expects and what the members expect and possibly even what the community that the church body sets in, expects.*

Do you think there is may be some added strain in the relationship in the pastor's life with all these expectations that may be realistic or unrealistic?

Pastor: *Undoubtedly, the answer to that is true. That there is a great deal of strain between, all that you just mentioned. I see the acronym (CCCC). What the church expects is one thing and that of course is to be there at all times to marry people, bury people, hold communion service, to counsel people. There's an endless amount of things that the church expects and of course the conference has its expectations also, which I believe basically is to make sure you represent the conference correctly. They don't want you to do something that's going to cause embarrassment to them or to the body of Christ. You have a certain professionalism you need to carry yourself with.*

The third C, after church and conference, is community; the community of course is expecting you to feed the hungry, cloth the naked and address all the community needs, things of that nature.

I think when we focus on those things the strain increases, because there's never ending point, I'm sure you know. The phone calls and letters asking you to speak here and pray there to do this. But I find there is a fourth C that we need to be concerned about, and that is what is Christ's concern.

If we get those things in the proper priority, and to me the priority would be Christ first, of course, the church second, conference third, and the community fourth. If we focus, as the Lord said, seek ye first the kingdom of God and his righteousness. If we focus on Christ's demands and what he wants, I find that the load becomes much lighter.

The challenge is to find that time for Christ. Personally I find that if I don't get it early in the morning, I'll probably miss it the rest of the day. But, if I get a good hour to two hours with Him in His word or on my knees, which may begin as early as 4:00 in the morning, if I get that, it is much better, but if I don't get that, then it's like a rat race, you're running and you never catch up.

Question: *That's very enlightening.*

How would you say you handled conflict? And would you say that, when pastor's personal convictions are threatened that conflict will arise?

Pastor: *First of all in handling conflict: after getting my Batchelor of Arts degree in Theology, I found a great deal of counseling was necessary, I felt totally inadequate to address the needs of the people. There is a certain amount of praying I could do, there's only a certain amount of Bible studies I could do and it was all good, but I felt that there was a lot of practical hands on things that I did not know and because of that I went back and got my Masters Degree in Psychology and Counseling. That's what prompted me to do it more than anything because these people came with very practical issues, and my answers were always on a spiritual nature and sometimes the nature [of the need] was not spiritual.*

I believe everything has a spiritual implication to it, but there were other concerns. When a person comes and says he hasn't been working for six months and his wife is thinking about leaving him and he's been praying and he's been studying, then there is some practical issue that needs to take place and by that I mean, does he have a resume made up, has he gone to any type of job interviews, learning techniques, and of course those might sound like common sense things but if you haven't had the training, then you don't know those things. So, that's why I went and got my Masters in

Counseling with an emphasis on chemical dependence, because there were a lot of people who had chemical problems; so those conflicts were many and varied. But the counseling degree did help me.

Question: *Did it help you deal with conflict?*

Pastor: *Oh yes, if anything, it gave me a certain amount of confidence, that I knew what I was talking about in those arenas. That added to the spiritual components I found complementing one another.*

The second part of your question was, "when a pastor feels his convictions are being threatened will that cause conflict?" Most definitely, the answer is yes there. I can give you a situation. I remember it distinctly. There was an individual who was wrestling with becoming a member of my church and was talking about leaving her current church. This person was trying to make up her mind; and she wanted to meet with me as well as her current pastor. So being a novice, I agreed to that, which I would never do again, by the way. So I met with her pastor. And we sat down and dialogued about various things, and of course, we came to no real conclusion. She ended up staying with the pastor she was with, because of course he knew the member much better than I did. And I found the person presenting certain things that threatened my convictions. I found myself getting somewhat irritated and aggravated with what the person was saying, because I felt my convictions were based on the word of God, but he probably felt the same way. He probably thought his convictions were based on the word of God also.

I've learned through that though, that the battle is not mine, the battle is the Lord's and the Lord will take care of it.

Question: **Would you say that conflict really adds to a pastor's stress load?**

Pastor: *Conflict adds to a pastor's stress load yes, but conflict also produces a certain character that the pastor would not receive if he didn't have those conflicts. So they can be very beneficial, while at the same time it can be heart wrenching and very painful.*

Question: **It sounds like you didn't recognize some signs early on in your ministry about not just your physical body, but maybe even your pastoral leadership. I'm speaking in general of course.**
Do you now feel more equipped to be able to

know when you need to back off or pace yourself in ministry?

Pastor: *Yes, I feel much more equipped and that's because I've gotten back to the strategy I mentioned to you before, by putting Christ first.*

It's really interesting that there's a statistic that I had heard of concerning Black pastors, now of course you realize being a pastor that the retirement age for Adventist ministers is 65 and you can't retire until you are 65 which means you do not get the benefits if you retire early.

The statistic that came to my attention was that the average Black minister in the Adventist church, died in his 50's, approximately 55 years old. Which meant to me that most Black ministers in the Adventist church never received any kind of retirement benefit and when I realized that, I asked, what am I doing here? I'm not going to retire at the pace I'm going if I'm the average minister, then I'm going to die before I'm 65. That caused me to step back and re-evaluate the pace in which I was running. Because I felt that I would run out of steam before I was 65. Not that I'm in this to retire, the Bible says you get three score and ten. I'd like my three score and ten.

Question: *What gave you the renewal you needed to*

say, I can do this again? That is, to pastor again?

Pastor: *First of all, when I stepped out of the pastorate, as I mentioned earlier, I didn't step out of ministry, I went back to teaching and what happened was I stopped teaching in public school and started teaching in a private school. I went there for one reason, and that was to read the Bible every day; and that of course is what you do in a private school teaching religion. Everyday I'm studying the life of Christ in the word of God in addition to teaching it to others. So, my main objective was my spiritual renewal, my spiritual awakening and now that I'm in my second year of doing this, it has happened exactly like I hoped it would.*

I went to get closer to the Lord and I have become closer to the Lord. Now in addition to that, renewal and revival in my own personal life, is something else that has happened to me in reflection. I thought about the training I received from school, from the conference, from the church level, and have come up with, "well now that the school has told me this is the way you should do it, and the conference has told me this is the way you should do it, and the church has said, this is the way to do it; and the community says, this is the way you should do it; I've taken all of their input, and

I have decided well okay, I see what you all have to say, let me see what God has to say." I decided to do it, and I have decided that in doing this new church I will work much, much less, the people will work much, much more, and the Holy Spirit will be the one that will direct all the energies.

At this point I feel that I can conceivably minister until the day I die, because I no longer feel that I'm the number one person. I am at the point of training everybody in the church to understand that they are all ministers. When someone is sick, I don't have to go to the hospital, anybody in the church has the same ability I do. They can go visit, keep the visit short, pray with the person, and encourage the person and leave. When someone is in prison, I don't have to be the only one to go to the jail. Anyone can go visit. So with this new found relationship with the Lord, I'm determined I'm not going to carry it, because I wasn't suppose to carry it to begin with.

Response to Pastor: *Sounds like you are relating to Moses and the counsel from his father-in-law Jethro in the Bible.*

Pastor: *Exactly, I might say there is a real problem here in working this kind of program especially pastoring with people who normally follow the traditional program.*

Question: *Which is?*

Pastor: *Which is, the pastor is the chief cook, baker, bottle washer, the pastor does it all. For some reason people feel they have to talk to the pastor, only the pastor can solve their problems. They can't talk to an elder, or deacon, or deaconess, for some reason the pastors have to be at this meeting and he just can't delegate and have someone report back to him. The pastor has to be the chairman of the church board, the pastor has to lead out in every function and of course, if the people have that traditional outlook and a pastor comes in and does it differently, they will consider the pastor, not the pastor. He's not pastoring they'll say. Where as if you are starting fresh and you train the people that this is the way we are going to do it, like Jethro told Moses, then it is a lot simpler to do it that way. I think a pastor would find it very, very hard in a traditional setting to do it, because it requires an opened mind and a willing spirit.*

Question: *Do you think pastoral burnout is a real issue in the Adventist church?*

Pastor: *There is no doubt that pastoral burnout is a real issue in the Adventist church; and also, I'm sure in other churches, but probably more so in the Adventist church, because of some of the peculiarities associated with the Adventist church. That being of course, not wearing jewelry, not wearing makeup, eating habits and things of that nature, pastors feel that stress. Which of course, and I hate to say it, I think hinders a person's relationship with Jesus Christ.*

If a person has a vibrant relationship with Jesus Christ then they will come to understand that there is a certain way to dress, you don't wear your skirts too short, and you don't go with your shirt opened and your chest exposed with hair on it. If the personal relationship with Christ is what it should be then, they will know that you don't dress like a Jezebel, and I say that sparingly. Because as the Bible says, let it not be of the outward adorning. But I think because of the peculiarity the pastor feels that these people need to look like "Christians" and we don't really know what a Christian looks like, because we can only tell a Christian by his/her heart.

Question: *Is mission the driving force in your ministry, particularly Matthew 28: 19 & 20?*

Pastor: *I can't really say that's my driving force. I can't really say, it used to be my driving force. Because I use to think that if we reached out and got a lot of souls then God would be glorified and the church would be edified; the more we baptized the more successful we were. I don't believe that anymore, we can have a thousand people in the church and it's possible that only ten know Christ.*

So, now my driving force, my mission, is to help people be like Christ. That is my driving force and I think if they become like Christ, then the second mission, "Go ye therefore and teach," would become a very simple matter. It would be very easy, if they have that relationship, because if they have that relationship with Christ they would want to tell somebody. Now my motivating force, my mission, is not to just baptize, it is not just to go and tell, but rather it's to help people become like Christ. If they become like Christ, the love, joy, happiness that they will experience will spill over into the communities, on their jobs, at school, wherever they go, they will have a sense of urgency to tell about their best friend and the lover of their soul.[1]

NOTES

Introduction

1   Robert H. Ramey, Jr. <u>Thriving in Ministry</u> (St. Louis: Chalice Press, 2000), 148-49.

2   Ellen G. White, <u>The Story of the Patriarchs and Prophets</u> (Mountain View, CA.: Pacific Press Publishing Association, 1913), 255.

Chapter 1

1   <u>Webster's New Ninth Collegiate Dictionary</u>, s.v. "burnout."

2   Ralph Douglas Haynes, "An Outline of Clergy Depression with Suggested Procedures and Strategies for Healing," D.Min. thesis., Fuller Theological Seminary, 1986, 138.

3   Ibid., 138-39.

4   Ibid., 139.

5   Brooks Faulkner, <u>Burnout in Ministry</u> (Nashville: Broadman Press, 1981), 38-39.

6   G. Lloyd Rediger, <u>Coping with Clergy Burnout</u> (Valley Forge: Judson Press, 1982), 18.

7   Harold D. Scott, "Personal Reflections on Pastoral Burnout", D.Min. thesis, Fuller Theological Seminary, 1994, 19.

8   Ibid.

9   John A. Sanford, <u>Ministry Burnout</u> (New York: Paulist Press, 1982), 1.

10   William H. Willimon, <u>Clergy and Laity Burnout</u> (Nashville: Abingdon Press, 1989), 25.

11   Ibid.

12   Ibid. 25-26.

13 Faulkner, 38-39.

14 Rediger, Coping with Clergy Burnout, 13.

15 Ibid., 15.

16 Ibid., 15-16.

17 Ibid.

18 Scripture cited by the writer of this project is from the King James Version, unless otherwise noted.

19 Jody Seymour, A Time for Healing: Overcoming the Perils of Ministry (Valley Forge: Judson Press, 1995), 3.

20 Ibid.

21 Ibid., 31.

22 Ibid.

23 Ibid., 32.

24 Cited in Seymour, 32.

25 Cited in Seymour, 32-33.

26 Seymour, 34.

27 Ibid.

28 Sanford, 83.

29 Pronoun references to God will be capitalized.

30 Sanford, 83-84.

31 Funk and Wagnalls Collegiate Dictionary, s. v. "renewal," "renew."

32 Ellen G. White, The Ministry of Healing (Boise: Idaho Pacific Press Publishing Association, 1905), 127.

33 Robert H. Ramey, Jr. Thriving in Ministry (St. Louis: Chalice Press, 2000), 148-49.

Chapter 2

1   Christina Maslach, <u>Professionals In Distress: Issues, Syndromes, and Solutions in Psychology</u>, ed. Richard R. Kilburg, Peter E. Nathan, Richard W. Thoreson, (Washington, D.C.: American Psychological Association, Inc., 1986), 62-63.

2   Seymour, 4.

3   Ibid.

4   Sanford, 44-45.

5   Ibid., 48.

6   Russell Burrill, <u>Revolution in the Church</u> (Fallbrook, Calif.: Hart Research Institute, 1993), 49.

7   Ellen G. White, <u>Testimonies for the Church</u>, vol. 7 (Mountain View, Calif.: Pacific Press Publishing Association, 1948), 20.

8   Burrill, 49.

9   Ellen G. White, <u>Gospel Workers</u> (Washington , D.C.: Review and Herald Publishing Association, 1915), 196.

10   Burrill, 49.

11   Ibid., 50.

12   Ibid.

13   White, <u>Testimonies for the Church</u>, 7:18.

14   Burrill, 50.

15   <u>Websters Ninth New Collegiate Dictionary</u>, s.v. "dilemma."

16   Willimon, 50-51.

17   Ibid., 50.

18   <u>Seventh-day Adventist Minister's Manual</u> (Silver Spring, MD: The Ministerial Association, 1992), 64.

19   Ibid.

20   Ibid., 65.

21   Don F. Neufeld and Julia Neuffer eds., "Development of
     Organization in SDA Church," Seventh-day Adventist Encyclopedia,.
     rev.ed., Commentary Reference Series, vol. 10(Hagerstown, Md:
     Review and Herald Publishing Association, 1986), 1042.

22   Ibid.

23   William E. Hulme, Managing Stress in Ministry (San Francisco:
     Harper & Row Publishers, 1985), 9.

24   SDA Minister's Manual, 59.

25   Ibid., 45.

26   Ibid., 46.

27   Ibid., 49.

28   Ibid., 47-48.

29   Andrew R. Irvine, Between Two Worlds: Understanding and
     Managing Clergy Stress (London: Mowbray, 1997), 9.

30   Ibid.

31   G. Lloyd Rediger, Clergy Killers: Guidance for Pastors and
     Congregations Under Attack (Louisville: Westminster John Knox
     ress, 1997), 35.

32   Dennis Wallstrom, Role Conflict and Burnout in the Ministry,
     Ph.D. diss., Fuller Theological Seminary, 1990 (Ann Arbor, Mich:
     UMI, 1991), 3.

33   Ibid.

34   Ibid., 3-4.

35   Rediger, Clergy Killers, 35.

36   Ibid.

37   H.B. London, Jr. and Neil B. Wiseman, Your Pastor is an
     Endangered Species (Wheaton, Ill.: Victor Books, 1996), 51.

38 Hulme, 8,10.

39 "London and Wiseman, Your Pastor is an Endangered Species, "Monday Morning" 18.

40 Ibid., 18-19.

41 Ibid., 19.

42 Ibid., 51.

43 Sanford, 32.

44 Willimon, 32.

45 Ibid., 34.

46 Sanford, 32-33.

47 Irvine, 8.

48 Ibid.

49 Sanford, 38.

50 Seventh-day Adventist Minister's Manual, 60.

51 Ibid.

52 Charles H. Cosgrove and Dennis D. Hatfield Church Conflict: The Hidden Systems Behind the Fights (Nashville: Abingdon Press, 1994), 20.

53 Ibid.

54 Rediger, Clergy Killers, 48.

55 Irvine, 7.

56 Ibid.

57 Ibid., 8.

58 Hulme, 5.

59 London and Wiseman, Your Pastor is an Endangered Species, 54.

60 Gini Graham Scott, Resolving Conflict with Others and within Yourself (Oakland, Calif.: New Harbinger Publications, 1990), 29-35.

61 London and Wiseman, <u>Your Pastor is an Endangered Species</u>, 54.

62 Robert H. Ramey, Jr. <u>Thriving in Ministry</u>. (St. Louis: Chalice Press, 2000), 89.

63 Hulme, 5.

64 Ibid.

65 Marshall Shelley, <u>Well-Intentioned Dragons: Ministering to Problem People in the Church</u> (Waco, Tex.: Word Books Publisher, 1985), 41.

66 Hulme, 6.

67 Shelley, 87.

68 Ibid.

69 Rediger, <u>Clergy Killers: Guidance for Pastor and Congregations Under Attack</u>, 48.

70 Ibid.

71 London and Wiseman, 54.

72 Ibid., 55.

73 Ibid.

Chapter 3

1 Don F. Neufeld and Julia Neuffer, eds., <u>Seventh-Day Adventist Encyclopedia</u>, "Pastor", rev. ed., Commentary Reference Series, vol. 10 (Hagerstown, Md.: Review and Herald Publishing Association, 1986), 1083.

2 Ibid.

3 <u>Seventh-day Adventist Church Manual,</u> Revised Edition 2000, 16th Edition (Hagerstown, Md.: Review and Herald Publishing Association, 2000), 137.

4   Ibid., 136.

5   Nuefeld and Nueffer eds., "Pastor," in <u>Seventh-day Adventist Encyclopedia</u>, Vol.10:1083.

6   Ibid.

7   White, <u>Gospel Workers</u>, 31.

8   Nuefeld and Neuffer, eds., "Ministers," in <u>Seventh-Day Adventist Encyclopedia</u>, Vol. 10: 900.

9   Ibid., vol. 10: 901.

10 Ibid.

11 Ibid.

12 Spiros Zodhiates, eds., <u>Lexical Aids To The New Testament</u> (Chattanooga, Tenn.: AMG Publishers, 1991), 1750.

13 <u>Seventh-Day Adventist Minister's Manual</u>, 28.

14 Burrill, 46-47.

15 Cited in Burrill, 47.

16 Burrill, 47.

17 Ibid.

18 Ibid.

19 Ibid., 47-48.

20 Ibid., 48.

21 Ibid.

22 Nuefeld and Neuffer, eds., "Ministers," in <u>Seventh-Day Adventist Encyclopedia</u>, Vol. 10: 900.

23 White, <u>Gospel Workers</u>, 13.

24 <u>Seventh-Day Adventist Minister's Manual</u>, 21.

25 Nuefeld and Neuffer, eds., "Ministers," in Seventh-Day Adventist Encyclopedia, Vol. 10: 900.

26 2 Timothy 4:7.

Chapter 4

1 Websters Third New International Dictionary of English Language Unabridged, s.v. "prevention."

2 London and Wiseman, Your Pastor is an Endangered Species, 17.

3 Faulkner, 46.

4 Ibid., 46-47.

5 Ibid., 51.

6 London, H. B. and Wiseman, Neil B. Pastors at Risk (Victor Books/SP Publications, Inc., 1993), 163.

7 Irvine, 155.

8 Cited in London and Wiseman, Your Pastor is an Endangered Species, 64-65.

9 Gospel Workers, 244.

10 Irvine, 152.

11 Ibid.

12 Ibid.

13 Ibid., 153.

14 Ibid., 154-155.

15 Hands, Donald R., and Wayne L. Fehr. Spiritual Wholeness for Clergy: A New Psychology of Intimacy with God, Self, and Others. Washington, D.C. Alban Institute, 1993. 58-59.

16 Ibid., 61.

17 Ibid., 61-62.

18 Ibid., 62.

19 Faulkner, 65-71.

20 White, Gospel Workers, 243-246.

21 Hands and Fehr, 71.

22 Ibid., 78.

23 Sanford, 105-114.

24 Rassieur, Charles L. Stress Management for Ministers. Philadelphia: Westminster Press, 1982. 52-53.

25 Sabbatical Manual, Southeastern California Conference of Seventh-day Adventists (Ministerial department 1989), 1-2.

26 Ibid., 3-4.

27 Ibid., 2-3.

28 Faulkner, 126.

29 Ibid.

30 London and Wiseman, Your Pastor is an Endangered Species, 64.

31 Barbara G. Gilbert, Who Ministers to Ministers? A Study of Support Systems for Clergy and Spouses (Washington, D.C.: Alban Institute, 1987), 50-51.

32 Irvine, 160.

33 Rediger, Coping With Clergy Burnout, 100-101.

34 London and Wiseman, Pastors at Risk, 232.

35 Ibid., 233.

Pastoral Interview

1 Ivan L. Williams, Sr., interview with pastor, 12 Dec. 1999.

BIBLIOGRAPHY

Ainsworth-Smith, Ian, and Peter Speck. Letting Go: Caring for the Dying and Bereaved. London: SPCK, 1982.

Barrett, Wayne C. Clergy Personal Finance. Nashville: Abingdon Press, 1990.

Barna, George, ed. Leaders on Leadership: Wisdom, Advice and Encouragement on the Art of Leading God's People. Ventura, Calif.: Regal Books, 1997.

Burrill, Russell. Revolution in the Church. Fallbrook, Calif.: Hart Research Institute, 1993.

Coate, Mary Anne. Clergy Stress: The Hidden Conflicts in Ministry. London: SPCK, 1989.

Cosgrove, Charles H., and Dennis D. Hatfield. Church Conflict: The Hidden Systems Behind the Fights. Nashville: Abingdon Press, 1994.

Davey, John. Burnout: Stress in Ministry. Harrisburg, Pa: Morehouse Publishing, 1995.

Eppler, Mark. Management Mess-Ups: 57 Pitfalls You Can Avoid. Franklin Lakes, N.J.: Career Press, 1997.

Faulkner, Brooks R. Burnout in Ministry. Nashville: Broadman Press, 1981.

Gilbert, Barbara G. Who Ministers to Ministers? A Study of Support Systems for Clergy and Spouses. Washington, D.C.: Alban Institute, 1987.

Golembiewski, Robert T. Phases in Burnout: Developments in Concepts and Applications. New York: Praeger, 1988.

Golembiewski, Robert T., Robert F. Munzenrider, and Jerry G. Stevenson. Stress in Organizations: Toward a Phase Model of Burnout. New York: Praeger Publishing, 1985.

Guinness Os, ed. Character Counts: Leadership Qualities in Washington, Wilberforce, Lincoln, and Solzhenitsyn. Grand Rapids: Baker Books, 1999.

Hands, Donald R., and Wayne L. Fehr. Spiritual Wholeness for Clergy: A New Psychology of Intimacy with God, Self, and Others. Washington, D.C. Alban Institute, 1993.

Hart, Archibald D. Coping with Depression in the Ministry and Other Helping Professions. Waco, Tex.: Word Books, 1984.

Holck, Manfred, Jr. Making It on a Pastor's Pay. Nashville: Abingdon Press, 1974.

Hulme, William E. Managing Stress in Ministry. San Francisco: Harper & Row Publishers, 1985.

Hull, Bill. The Disciple Making Pastor. Old Tappan, N.J.: Fleming H.Revell, 1988.

Irvine, Andrew R. Between Two Worlds: Understanding and Managing Clergy Stress. London: Mowbray, 1997.

Leas, Speed B. Creative Leadership Series: Leadership & Conflict. Ed. Lyle E. Schaller. Nashville, Tenneessee: Abingdon, 1982.

Lee, Harris W. Effective Church Leadership: A Practical Sourcebook. Minneapolis: Augsburg, 1989.

Littauer, Florence. How to Get Along with Difficult People. updated and expanded ed. Eugene, Ore.: Harvest House Publishers, 1999.

London, H. B., Jr., and Neil B. Wiseman. Pastors at Risk. Colorado Springs, CO: Victor Books/SP Publications, Inc., 1993.

London, H. B., Jr., and Neil B. Wiseman. Your Pastor is an Endangered Species. Wheaton, Ill.: Victor Books, 1996.

Mace, David, and Vera Mace What's Happening to Clergy Marriages? Nashville: Abingdon Press, 1980.

Madden, James P., ed. Loneliness: Issues of Emotional Living In an Age of Stress for Clergy and Religious: The Second Boston Psychotheological Symposium. Whitinsville, Mass.: Affirmation Books, 1977.

Malakh, Ayala Pines, and Elliot Aronson. Career Burnout: Causes and Cures. New York: Free Press, 1988.

Maslach, Christina. Burnout: The Cost of Caring. New York: Prentice Hall Press, 1982.

Maslach, Christina. Professionals In Distress: Issues, Syndromes, and Solutions in Psychology. Ed. Richard R. Kilburg, Peter E. Nathan, Richard W. Thoreson. Washington, D.C.: American Psychological Association, Inc., 1986.

Markham, Ursula. How to Deal with Difficult People. London: Thorsons, 1993.

Maxwell, John C. The 21 Irrefutable Laws of Leadership: Follow Them and People Will Follow You. Nashville: Thomas Nelson Publishers, Inc., 1998.

Menking, Stanley J. Helping Laity Help Others. Philadelphia: Westminster Press, 1984.

Mills, Edgar W., and John P. Koval. Stress in the Ministry. Washington, D.C.: Ministry Studies Board, 1971.

Millican, Haviland H. Teamwork without Tears. Nashville: Christian Educators Fellowship, The United Methodist Church, 1968.

Neufeld, Don F., and Julia Neuffer, eds. Seventh-Day Adventist Bible Students Sourcebook. Commentary Reference Series, vol. 9. Washington, D.C.: Review and Herald Publishing Association, 1962.

Neufeld, Don F., and Julia Neuffer, eds. Seventh-Day Adventist Encyclopedia. Rev. ed. Commentary Reference Series, vol. 10. Washington, D.C.: Review and Herald Publishing Association, 1976.

The Bible. New International Version.

O'Connor, Brian P., Daniel J. Cherico, Carole E. Smith Torres, Austin H. Kutscher, Jacob Goldberg, and Karin M. Muraszko, eds., The Pastoral Role in Caring for the Dying and Bereaved; Pragmatic and Ecumenical. New York: Praeger Publishers, 1986.

Olsen, V. Norskov. Myth & Truth Church, Priesthood & Ordination. Riverside, Calif.: Loma Linda University Press, 1990.

Oswald, Roy M. Clergy Self-Care: Finding a Balance for Effective Ministry. Washington, D.C.: Alban Institute, 1991.

Oswald, Roy M., Gail D. Hinand, William Chris Hobgood, and Barton M. Lloyd. New Visions for the Long Pastorate. Washington, D.C.: Alban Institute, 1983.

Pannell, Nancy. Being a Minister's Wife...and Being Yourself. Nashville: Broadman Press, 1993.

Pappas, Anthony G. Pastoral Stress: Sources of tension Resources for transformation. Bethesda, Md.: Alban Institute, 1995.

Ramey, Robert H., Jr. Thriving in Ministry. St. Louis: Chalice Press, 2000.

Rassieur, Charles L. Christian Renewal: Living Beyond Burnout. Philadelphia: Westminster Press, 1984.

Rassieur, Charles L. Stress Management for Mininsters. Philadelphia: Westminster Press, 1982.

Rediger, G. Lloyd. Clergy Killers: Guidance for Pastors and Congregations under Attack. Louisville: Westminster John Knox Press, 1997.

Rediger, G. Lloyd. Coping with Clergy Burnout. Valley Forge: Judson Press, 1982.

Rhodes, John. Success Secrets for Pastors. Silver Spring, Md: The Ministerial Association, General Conference of Seventh-day Adventists, 1973.

Ross, Charlotte. Who is the Minister's Wife? A Search for Personal Fulfillment. Philadelphia: Westminster Press, 1980.

Ryan, James R. Scriptural Images of Stress in the Ministry for Senior Ministers of Large Congregations. Bethesda, Md: Alban Institute, 1989.

Sanford, John A. Ministry Burnout. New York: Paulist Press, 1982.

Scott, Gini Graham. Resolving Conflict with Others and within Yourself. Oakland, Calif.: New Harbinger Publications, 1990.

Seventh-Day Adventist Church Manual. 15th ed. Hagerstown, Md.: Review and Herald Publishing Association, 1995.

Seventh-Day Adventist Minister's Manual. Silver Spring, Md.: The Ministerial Association, 1992.

Seymour, Jody. A Time for Healing: Overcoming the Perils of Ministry. Valley Forge: Judson Press, 1995.

Shelley, Marshall. Well-Intentioned Dragons: Ministering to Problem People in the Church. Waco, Tex.: Word Books Publisher, 1985.

Swindoll, Charles R. Growing Strong in the Seasons of Life. Portland, Ore.: Multnomah Press, 1983.

Taylor, Barbara Brown. When God is Silent. Boston, Massachusetts: Cowley
Publications, 1998.

Veninga, Robert L., and James P. Spradley. The Work / Stress Connection: How to Cope with Job Burnout. Boston: Little, Brown, 1981.

Wareing, Ernest Clyde. Critical Hours in the Preachers Life. New York: George H. Doran Company, 1923.

Weiser, Conrad W. Healers: Harmed and Harmful. Minneapolis: Fortress Press, 1994.

Were, Louis F. The Certainty of the Third Angel's Message. Berrien Springs, Mich.: First Impressions, 1979.

White, Ellen G. The Acts of the Apostles. Mountain View, Calif.: Pacific Press Publishing Association, 1911.

White, Ellen G. Diet and Foods. Washington, D.C.: Review and Herald Publishing Association, 1938.

White, Ellen G. Evangelism. Washington, D.C.: Review and Herald Publishing Association, 1946.

White, Ellen G. Gospel Workers. Washington, D.C.: Review and Herald Publishing Association, 1915.

White, Ellen G. The Ministry of Healing. Boise, Idaho: Pacific Press Publishing Association, 1905.

White, Ellen G. The Story of the Patriarchs and Prophets. Mountain View, Calif.: Pacific Press Publishing Association, 1913.

White, Ellen G. The Story of Prophets and Kings. Mountain View, Calif.: Pacific Press Publishing Association, 1917.

White, Ellen G. Temperance. Mountain View, Calif.: Pacific Press Publishing Association, 1949.

White, Ellen G. Testimonies for the Church. Vol. 7. Mountain View, Calif.: Pacific Press Publishing Association, 1948.

White, Ellen G. Testimonies on Sexual Behavior, Adultery, and Divorce. Silver Spring, Md: The Ellen White Estate, 1989.

Willimon, William H. Clergy and Laity Burnout. Nashville: Abingdon Press, 1989.

Wimberly, Edward P. Recalling Our Own Stories: Spiritual Renewal for Religious Caregivers. San Francisco: Jossey-Bass Publishers, 1997.

Zodhiates, Spiros. eds., Lexical Aids To The New Testament. Chattanooga, Tenn.: AMG Publishers, Inc., 1991.

Articles

Hanson, David. "War of the Baseball Caps." Leadership: A Practical Journal for Church Leaders 19, no. 2 (1998) : 54-59.

Henry, Jim. "Character Forged from Conflict." Leadership: A Practical Journal for Church Leaders 19, no. 2 (1998) : 20-26.

McBurney, Louis. "North American Guide to Church Dragons." Leadership: A Practical Journal for Church Leaders 19, no. 2 (1998) : 34-38.

Neufeld, Don F., and Julia Neuffer, eds. "Development of Organization in SDA Church." In Seventh-Day Adventist Encyclopedia, 1042. Rev. ed. Commentary Reference Series, vol. 10. Washington, D.C.: Review and Herald Publishing Association, 1976.

Neufeld, Don F., and Julia Neuffer, eds. "Ministers." In Seventh-Day Adventist Encyclopedia, 900. Rev. ed. Commentary Reference Series, vol. 10. Washington, D.C.: Review and Herald Publishing Association, 1976.

Neufeld, Don F., and Julia Neuffer, eds. "Pastor." In Seventh-Day Adventist Encyclopedia, 1083. Rev. ed. Commentary Reference Series, vol. 10. Washington, D.C.: Review and Herald Publishing Association, 1976.

Preston, Gary D. "Resisting the Urge to Hit Back." Leadership: A Practical Journal for Church Leaders 19, no. 2 (1998) : 60-64.

Other Sources

Blackmon, Richard Allen. The Hazards of the Ministry. Ph.D. diss., Fuller Theological Seminary, 1984. Ann Arbor, Mich.: UMI, 1985.

Brown, Nathan Cunningham. The Influence of Social Networks on Burn-out in the Ministry. Ph.D. diss., Fuller Theological Seminary, 1985.

Haynes, Ralph Douglas. "An Outline of Clergy Depression: with Suggested Procedures and Strategies for Healing." D.Min. thesis., Fuller Theological Seminary, 1986.

Lucht, Gary C. Priorities for Ministry: A Strategy for Balance in the Life of the Pastor. D.Min. thesis., Fuller Theological Seminary, Ann Arbor, Mich: UMI,1988.

Sabbatical Manual. Southeastern California Conference of Seventh-day Adventists Ministerial department. 1989. Riverside, CA.

Scott, Harold D. "Personal Reflections on Pastoral Burnout." D.Min. thesis., Fuller Theological Seminary, 1994.

Valenzuela, Alfonso. An Ecosystemic Analysis of Marital Satisfaction in Seventh-Day Adventist Clergy Families. Ph.D. diss., Fuller Theological Seminary, 1991. Ann Arbor, Mich.: UMI, 1991.

Wallstrom, Dennis . Role Conflict and Burnout in the Ministry. Ph.D. diss., Fuller Theological Seminary, 1990. Ann Arbor, Mich.: UMI, 1991.

MORE ABOUT THE AUTHOR

Dr. Ivan L. Williams, Sr. was born in Winston-Salem, North Carolina and grew up in Atlanta, Georgia. He graduated from Oakwood College, in Huntsville, Alabama, with an Associate of Science degree in Communications in 1985 and a Bachelor of Arts degree in Theology in 1986. In 1988 he graduated from Andrews University, in Berrien Springs, Michigan, with a Masters of Divinity and from Commissioned Officer Training School USAF in 1996. In 2002, Williams graduated from Squadron Officer School Air University in Residence and from Claremont School of Theology, in Claremont, California with a Doctor of Ministry degree. His dissertation dealt with pastoral burnout and renewal in Seventh-day Adventist ministry.

Currently, Dr. Williams serves as the senior pastor of the Capitol City SDA Church in Sacramento, California. He serves as a Chaplain for the California State Assembly, and as a Chaplain (Major) for the 129th California Air National Guard Rescue Wing. He is president of Brighter Hope Ministries, Inc. and can be heard nationwide over the Lifetalk radio network.

His pastoral ministry spans over eighteen years, and has included churches such as Northeast SDA Church in Charlotte, North Carolina, First Ridgeland and Beaufort Temple SDA Churches in South Carolina, Kansas Avenue SDA Church in Riverside, California, Juniper Avenue SDA Church in Fontana, California, and Maranatha SDA Church in San Diego, California. Dr. Williams serves as a board member for the Pacific Union Conference Executive Committee of the Seventh-day Adventist Church.

His awards and achievements include: Certified Prepare and Enrich Marital Counselor; evangelist/founder of a new church, Beaufort Temple SDA Church in Beaufort, South Carolina; Pastor of the Year Award in Southeastern California Conference of Seventh-day Adventists; writer of lyrics and songs; author of *Keep the Flame Burning in Your Ministry*; television host of Brighter Hope on RCC-TV Sacramento, California. Dr. Williams has also traveled and spoken throughout North America and around the world.

Dr. Williams enjoys radio broadcasting, reading, preaching, barbering, basketball, golfing, swimming, family time, giving people hope and teaching them to live a balanced Christian life. He is married to Kathleen Scott Williams, and they are the proud parents of their daughter, Imani, and their son, Ivan, II.

PERSONAL RENEWAL NOTES

PERSONAL RENEWAL NOTES

PERSONAL RENEWAL NOTES

PERSONAL RENEWAL NOTES